Essential Life Skills Every Teen Should Know!

The Ultimate Guide for Young Adults, Essential Habits for Managing Money, Cooking, Cleaning, Job Hunting, Decision-Making and Achieving Independence.

Chloe J. Boulding

Copyright

Table of Contents

Part I

Introduction and Overview

Chapter 1

Introduction: Essential Life Skills Every Teen Should Know!

Welcome to "Essential Life Skills Every Teen Should Know!" a guide designed specifically for you, the teenager, navigating the thrilling yet challenging journey of adolescence. A lot of development and change takes place throughout these formative years. You're making decisions, forming bonds, and developing a sense of self that will define your future. It's an exciting journey with lots of unknowns and potential obstacles. This guide is meant to be a dependable friend, here to help you through the exciting adventure ahead.

Why You Need This Book

Before we get into the meat of this guide, it's important to answer the question, "Why do you need this book?" After all, there are a ton of other resources out there, so you might be wondering what makes this one special. Some very good arguments are as follows.

Tailored to You

The advice in "Essential Life Skills Every Teen Should Know!" is tailored to you and your life. It recognizes the difficulties of being an adolescent and provides helpful guidance for overcoming them.

Comprehensive Guidance

Everything from self-improvement and relationships to money management and long-term planning is included in this comprehensive guide. It's a one-stop shop for learning all the basics of life.

Relatable and Engaging

We get that learning new life skills and improving oneself via reading may not sound particularly exciting. That's why we packed this book with real-world anecdotes, applicable examples, and fun exercises to keep you interested and inspired.

Empowerment

We hope that you'll get the tools you need to not only flourish as a teenager but also to launch into a successful and rewarding adult life.

A Trusted Companion

Consider this guide your reliable companion. When you need help the most, it will be there to guide you and reassure you. This book will show you that you have friends and allies along for the ride.

As we go off on our adventure, keep in mind that you control your fate. Become the finest possible version of yourself with every choice you make, talent you master, and life lessons you absorb. "Essential Life Skills Every Teen Should Know" is here to help you through every difficulty in life, from overcoming obstacles to improving yourself and your relationships.

The next chapters are filled with actionable advice and engaging exercises designed to provide you with the skills you need to successfully manage the challenges of adolescence. Let's launch ourselves on this amazing journey of introspection, development, and agency. This guide will help you reach your greatest potential and take control of your destiny.

Part II

Personal Skills and Self-Awareness

Chapter 2

Being a Teenager: The Challenge and the Adventure

Adolescence is a special and formative time of life, full of experiences and opportunities that mold and develop a person. It's a period of development, change, and discovery that may bring forth a wide range of emotions. What it means to be a teenager, the difficulties you may face, and the opportunities that await you are the subjects of this chapter.

The Teenage Experience

The adolescent years are a tremendous time of development and change. You will experience profound changes in your body, emotions, and mind throughout this period. As you forge your way toward autonomy and individuality, these transformations may be both thrilling and bewildering.

Physical Changes

The physical changes that take place during adolescence are one of the most striking features of this developmental stage. As your body develops rapidly, you may notice changes like:

Puberty:

Secondary sexual traits are developed throughout the biological process of puberty. Ages 8-13 for females and 10-14 for boys are common onset ages. Changes like as the development of breasts, a deeper voice, and the appearance of facial and body hair will occur during this period.

Growth Spurts:

As your body undergoes a growth spurt, you may notice that you are suddenly much taller than your peers. Adjusting to your new physique during a growth spurt is natural but can be uncomfortable.

Hormonal Changes:

Adolescent hormones are crucial to your mental and physical health. Mood swings, acne, and altered body odor are all symptoms of hormonal shifts.

Brain Development:

The parts of the brain responsible for making decisions and controlling impulses are still maturing during adolescence. This is why it might be hard for you to make good decisions occasionally.

Emotional Rollercoaster

Teenagers' emotional experiences tend to be complex and strong. On any one day, you might experience a wide range of emotions, from elation to rage to depression and back again. These feelings indicate that you are maturing and expanding your capacity for empathy.

Keep in mind that these feelings are normal and acceptable. They are essential to your humanity. Learning constructive methods of dealing with and expressing one's emotions is equally important. We will learn techniques for self-control and introspection as we proceed through this guide.

Cognitive Growth

Your brain develops further during your teenage years. You'll begin to engage in more abstract thought, question established assumptions, and form your own set of values and priorities. Your maturation into an adult requires you to have the capacity to think critically and independently.

Challenges of Adolescence

Being a teenager is a thrilling experience, but it also has its difficulties. Recognizing these difficulties and realizing that you are not alone in confronting them is crucial. Many young people face comparable challenges as they try to mature. Problems of a typical kind include:

Academic Pressure

As a teenager, you may feel a lot of pressure to succeed in school. Planning for your future education and profession may have to take a back seat to the demands of schoolwork, tests, and extracurricular activities. Finding a good equilibrium and asking for help when you need it are necessities in times of high strain.

Peer Relationships

When you're a teenager, your friendships with your peers are more important than ever. Peer pressure, the need to fit in, and the dynamics of your friendships might shift. Managing these relationships is difficult, but it's a great chance to grow your social skills and make some great connections.

Identity Exploration

The process of self-discovery often involves challenging long-held assumptions about who you are and what you value. This time of introspection and discovery is essential to healthy development. You can learn more about yourself and the things that are important to you.

Independence and Responsibility

Adolescence is a time of growing maturity and responsibility. You'll start to take charge of your own life and make decisions about things like time management and how you spend your energy. This increased independence comes with the responsibility of making wise choices.

Peer Pressure

Adolescents often struggle with the effects of peer pressure on topics such as substance usage, romantic relationships, and social conformity. One of the most important skills for dealing with social pressure is learning how to make decisions that are consistent with your beliefs and aspirations.

Emotional Rollercoaster

Sometimes the intensity of feelings throughout adolescence might be too much to handle. The ability to regulate and deal with such feelings is essential to one's psychological health.

Family Dynamics

You may have tensions at home as you begin to establish your individuality. Adolescence brings about these disagreements since everyone in the family is adjusting to new responsibilities and expectations.

Embracing the Adventure

Although these obstacles may appear to be insurmountable, it is essential to keep in mind that being a teenager is also an exciting experience that is packed with chances for one's development and self-discovery. Your personality will be formed and you will be well-prepared for the years to come thanks to the experiences you have throughout these years.

Chapter 3

Identity and Self-Awareness: Who Are You, Really?

The question "Who am I?" This inquiry is fundamental to your development as a young adult. Philosophers, poets, and intellectuals have all wondered about this, and now it's your chance to dig into the topic. During your adolescence, you'll do a lot of soul-searching and learn a lot about who you are as a person.

The Quest for Identity

The idea of identity is intricate and multidimensional. It includes many aspects of who you are, not just your views and ideals. What makes you, you, is your set of qualities and experiences. Your sense of self changes as you gain experience and insight into who you are and the world around you.

Self-Concept

Your self-concept is fundamental to who you are. This is your internalized picture of your skills, attractiveness, and value. Factors like your upbringing, life experiences, and relationships with people all play a role in shaping your sense of self.

Imagine that your self-concept is like a blueprint or mental picture of who you are. It determines how you see yourself and the world. If you have a healthy view of yourself, you're more inclined to face adversity head-on. Conversely, if you have a poor image of yourself, you may struggle with self-doubt and low self-esteem.

The Search for Authenticity

When you're a teenager, you can start to question the roles and expectations that others (including society, family, and peers) have set for you. This is a natural and necessary stage of maturation. It's how you figure out what you care about and whether anything is in line with your core values.

Finding your true identity, the one you hold when you're not attempting to please others is central to the pursuit of authenticity. Being authentic means prioritizing your own needs and goals over those of others.

Influences on Identity

Your sense of self doesn't materialize in a void. Several internal and environmental factors form it. Recognizing these factors helps shed light on your identity and decision-making processes.

Internal Influences

The term "internal influences" refers to those that are generated from inside. For example:

Genetics:

Your temperament and inclinations toward particular actions may have their origins in your genes.

Personal Experiences:

Your identity is heavily influenced by the sum of your life experiences. Your distinctive outlook on life is shaped by your experiences, both good and bad.

Values and Beliefs:

The principles by which you make decisions and identify what matters to you are rooted in your values and beliefs. Family, culture, and introspection are common sources of these.

Interests and Passions:

The things you like to do and study may tell others a lot about who you are. Your passions may be a window into who you are, whether they be in the arts, athletics, science, or something else completely.

External Influences

Some examples of things you can attribute to the outside world are:

Family:

The people you grow up with have a major impact on who you become. They are the source of your first morals, ethics, and cultural understanding. The expectations and backing of your loved ones might have an impact on the decisions you make.

Peers:

The people you hang out with can have a significant effect on who you become. The people around you have a significant impact on whether or not you will acquire particular behaviors or interests.

Culture and Society:

Your identity is formed in part by the greater cultural and socioeconomic environment in which you find yourself. Your perception of yourself and the people around you is influenced by cultural conventions, expectations, and the media.

Media and Technology:

Your opinions and values might be influenced by the movies, music, and social media you take in. Understanding how different forms of media may affect one's sense of identity is crucial.

Self-Discovery Activities

The following exercises might serve as a springboard for your quest for self-knowledge:

Journaling

Keeping a journal is a great approach to examine your inner life and get insight. Don't be hesitant to delve into your innermost ideas and feelings; write frequently.

Values Assessment

Determine what you hold most dear in life and make it your guiding principle. You may discover evaluations and tools online to assist you figure out what you truly value in life.

Self-Reflection

Dedicate some time to thinking about your life. Pondering such queries as "What are my strengths and weaknesses?" is a good place to start. and "What am I working toward in the long run?"

Explore New Activities

Experimenting with new pursuits might help you learn more about who you are. Taking up a new hobby, whether it's painting, volunteering, or joining a sports team, maybe a rewarding experience.

Seek Feedback

Get honest assessments of your strengths and development needs from loved ones. There are moments when other people can see the best in us even when we can't.

Keep in mind that learning about oneself is a continual process. Your sense of self will develop more as you learn and grow. If you approach it with an attitude of openness and exploration, you'll discover that learning about yourself is an ongoing journey.

Chapter 4

Understanding and Improving Self-Confidence: Your Personal Superpower

Envision entering a room full of individuals, all having their own set of skills and experiences to offer. You are surrounded by people who are confident, strong, and fearless. Why are they different? It's a trait commonly known as self-confidence, and it makes all the difference in how one handles difficulties and chances in life.

The Power of Self-Confidence

Confidence in oneself is having faith in one's skills, judgment, and value. Confidence is knowing you can handle challenges and accomplish your goals. Confidence isn't about never making mistakes or doubting yourself; it's about trusting in your ability to develop and succeed despite setbacks.

The Role of Self-Confidence

Confidence is like a superpower because of the many ways in which it may improve your life.

Achievement:

When you have faith in yourself, you're more inclined to push yourself to the limit in pursuit of your goals. The will to achieve is fueled by your faith in yourself.

Resilience:

Having confidence in yourself makes it easier to recover from disappointments. It's what helps you dig deep when things get tough.

Relationships:

Confidence is a great asset in social situations. Confidence boosts your odds of having fruitful conversations, setting good boundaries, and making positive relationships.

Mental Health:

Confidence in oneself is correlated with psychological health. It can help you feel less stressed and down, giving you a more upbeat perspective on life.

Decision-Making:

People who are secure in their abilities tend to make better choices. They are confident in their decisions and rarely second-guess themselves.

The Confidence-Competence Loop

Confidence and skill go hand in hand in fascinating ways. Confidence may affect how others see your competence, which relates to your real talents and abilities. The confidence-competence loop describes this feedback loop.

Positive Loop:

Confidence encourages action, which in turn increases one's chances of becoming skilled in one's chosen area. If you think you have what it takes to be a sports star, for instance, you'll work hard to become that way.

Negative Loop:

On the flip side, insecurity might prevent you from taking risks and accomplishing goals. Because of this, you may be less likely to gain experience and confidence.

This feedback loop emphasizes the significance of fostering and sustaining self-assurance, making it crucial to comprehend. When you believe in yourself, you're more likely to take initiative, gain wisdom from your mistakes, and develop further.

Building Self-Confidence

The uplifting news is that one's level of self-confidence may change over time. It's a talent that may grow with practice and attention over time. The following are some methods that might assist you in establishing and enhancing your self-confidence:

Set Realistic Goals

To get started, you should give yourself attainable goals. These objectives should be difficult to achieve but not insurmountable. You will acquire confidence in your ability to establish goals for yourself and achieve them as you go toward completing them.

Celebrate Small Wins

Recognize and honor your accomplishments, no matter how insignificant they may appear to be, and celebrate them. Recognizing your accomplishments, no matter how large or small, may help you feel more confident and increase your self-esteem.

Face Your Fears

Put yourself in uncomfortable situations to force you to venture beyond your comfort zone. Confronting your phobias and challenging yourself with new experiences might help you become more aware of your talents and advantages.

Practice Self-Compassion

Treat yourself with compassion and empathy at all times. Stay away from severe self-criticism and critical internal monologues. Be kind and compassionate to yourself in the same way that you would be to a friend.

Develop Competence

Put in the effort to expand your knowledge and capabilities in the areas that are most meaningful to you. Your self-assurance in those domains will naturally grow to match your increased competence as time goes on.

Embrace Failure

Failing at anything is an inevitable aspect of life, but it can also be used as a learning and development opportunity. Instead of being something to be feared, failure should be seen as a necessary step on the path to achievement.

Surround Yourself with Positivity

Put yourself in the company of individuals who will encourage and inspire you. A solid basis for self-confidence may be established via the cultivation of healthy relationships.

Visualization

Imagine yourself becoming successful. Imagine reaching your objectives while simultaneously experiencing feelings of self-assurance and competence. Do this for a few minutes every day.

Accept Imperfection

Keep in mind that none of us are flawless. Accept yourself as you are and realize that the flaws you have are a part of what makes you special and human. Embrace them.

Practices for Fostering Confidence

Let's do a little bit of work to put these ideas into practice. Here are some questions for you to answer in a notepad or on your computer.

1. What are three achievements you're proud of in your life so far, no matter how small?

2. Think about a goal you've been wanting to pursue but have hesitated to start. Write down that goal.

3. Break down that goal into smaller, actionable steps. What's the first step you can take today?

4. List three qualities or skills you possess that you're confident about.

5. Think of a role model or someone you admire. What qualities or characteristics do they possess that you would like to develop or embody?

The work here is only the first step. You will have several chances to boost your confidence as you move through puberty and beyond. Take advantage of these openings by keeping a positive attitude and trusting in your abilities.

Chapter 5

Building Resilience: How to Bounce Back Like a Pro

As a teenager, you've probably already experienced a wide range of positive and negative feelings and events throughout your life. Your ability to develop resilience is a key life skill that will see you through difficult times and emerge stronger on the other side.

What Is Resilience?

The capacity to overcome difficulties and failures is known as resilience. It's not about dodging challenges, but rather about finding creative solutions to them. Resilient people can weather the challenges of life and emerge stronger on the other side.

The Resilience Mindset

The ability to bounce back from adversity depends on one's frame of mind. Some essential features of a resilient outlook are as follows:

Positive Outlook:

Those who are resilient usually look at the bright side of things. They have faith in their abilities to persevere and ultimately succeed.

Adaptability:

Being pliable and malleable is essential to resilience. It's about realizing that you're capable of adapting to and thriving in different environments.

Problem-Solving:

Skills in problem-solving are crucial to resilience. Resilient people take a logical approach when confronted with adversity, looking for ways to overcome it rather than wallowing in self-pity.

Emotional Regulation:

The capacity to control and moderate one's emotions is a key component of resilience. It's about keeping your cool when things become rough and not letting your feelings get the best of you.

Social Support:

Building resilience requires support from others. Having somebody you can turn to for advice and comfort in times of need is invaluable.

The Importance of Resilience

As a teenager, why do you need to be so resilient? The reasons include the following:

Building Character:

Building one's character requires a dose of resilience. It's a great way to build stamina, resolve, and determination.

Coping with Change:

The adolescent years are marked by profound transformation, from maturing physically to taking on increased independence and adult responsibilities. Having the ability to adjust to these shifts depends on your level of resilience.

Navigating School and Relationships:

Success in school, resistance to negative peer pressure, and the ability to weather the ups and downs of friendships and love relationships are all aided by a strong dose of resilience.

Preparing for the Future:

The capacity to recover quickly from disappointments will serve you well in many contexts, including your academic and professional endeavors.

Building Resilience

You are not necessarily born with the ability to bounce back from adversity; rather, it is a skill that can be developed and honed over time. The following are some ways that might assist you in developing your resilience:

Develop a Growth Mindset

Adopt what is known as a "growth mindset," which is the concept that you can learn and improve as a result of the events and obstacles you face. Embrace the belief that failures are just chances to grow as a person and in your abilities.

Build Strong Relationships

Foster the relationships you have with other people. During difficult times, having a network of friends and mentors who are there to support and encourage you may serve as a priceless safety net.

Cultivate Emotional Intelligence

Develop an awareness of your feelings and the skills necessary to properly control them. Understanding your own emotions as well as those of others is a key component of emotional intelligence, which may help you strengthen your relationships and your ability to bounce back from setbacks.

Set Realistic Goals

Make sure that the objectives you set for yourself can be achieved by breaking them down into more manageable chunks. Even when you are confronted with difficulties, this might help you keep your sense of purpose and direction intact.

Practice Self-Care

You should pay attention to both your physical and emotional health. Make it a top priority to engage in activities that will help you relax, regain your energy, and keep up a healthy lifestyle.

Develop Problem-Solving Skills

When confronted with a difficulty, one should tackle it methodically. Determine the nature of the issue at hand, consider the many options open to you, and then take the necessary steps to handle it.

Seek Support

When assistance is required, do not be reluctant to seek it out. Seeking help, whether from a trusted friend or family member, a member of one's own family, or a counselor, is not a show of weakness but rather of strength.

Practice Resilience-Building Activities

Participate in pursuits that will test your resiliency and stretch your muscles in new ways. This could entail attempting new things, taking on leadership responsibilities, or volunteering to assist people in need.

A Resilience-Building Exercise

The following is a starting point for developing resilience:

The Resilience Journal

Open a notebook or start a new document digitally, and label it "Resilience Journal." This notebook is for recording thoughts and feelings as they pertain to developing resilience. Here's the first step:

Identify Challenges:

List three recent difficulties you've had to overcome. Anything from a particularly challenging job to a conflict with a close friend might fall under this category.

Reflect on Your Response:

Think about your approach to overcoming each obstacle. How optimistic were you about the situation? Did you ask for assistance when you needed it? Did you manage to figure it out?

Growth Opportunities:

Think about the lessons you've picked up along the way. Have you developed any new abilities? What would you do differently the next time you were in a similar situation?

Set Resilience Goals:

After giving it some thought, decide on one or two objectives that will help you become more resilient. You may, for instance, resolve to adopt a more optimistic perspective while dealing with difficulties or to actively look for help.

Keeping a Resilience Journal is an excellent way to document your efforts toward being more resilient and to discover what works best for you along the way. Be patient and compassionate to yourself as you attempt to build resilience; it's a talent that takes time to master.

Part III

Social Skills and Relationships

Chapter 6

Social Skills: How to Make and Keep Friends

The value of friendship may be measured by the amount of happiness, strength, and depth it brings into our lives. When you're a teenager, you're at an age where developing and keeping healthy friendships is an essential component of your overall growth as a person. Learning how to make friends and retain them is not only about finding company; it is also about learning key social skills that will serve you well throughout your whole life.

The Value of Friendship

Many aspects of your life may be improved by the cultivation of friendship, including but not limited to the following:

Emotional Support

In times of difficulty, having friends by your side may be a great support system. They provide support in the form of empathy as well as an ear to listen to and a shoulder to lean on.

Shared Experiences

Your friends will be there to rejoice and celebrate with you in your successes. They make the best parts of life that much more delightful to experience.

Fun and Laughter

Your days will be more enjoyable and full of laughter if you have friends. They are your companions on journeys of discovery and exploration.

Growth and Learning

Friends are the conduit via which you may gain exposure to novel concepts, points of view, and experiences. They teach you about the world as well as about yourself in the process.

Reduced Stress

Maintaining healthy relationships can help lower stress levels and improve mental and emotional well-being.

Building Social Skills

Having strong social skills is essential to maintaining lasting connections. Because you have these talents, you will be able to start and keep healthy connections with other people. The following are some of the most important social skills for forming and maintaining friendships:

Communication

The key to a healthy and fulfilling friendship is clear and consistent two-way communication. It requires being an engaged listener, being able to articulate oneself well, and having an awareness of nonverbal clues. When you practice active listening, you give the person who is speaking your undivided attention and you communicate your opinions and feelings openly while maintaining a courteous demeanor.

Empathy

The capacity to comprehend and identify with the emotions of another person is referred to as empathy. Being sympathetic enables you to form deeper, more meaningful connections with your friends. Make an effort to see things from the point of view of your friends and be there for them when they need help.

Cooperation

When both sides collaborate and are willing to compromise when it is required, a friendship will flourish. Maintain a collaborative mindset and show consideration for the requirements and viewpoints of your pals. The tie that exists between friends may be strengthened via cooperation.

Conflict Resolution

It is inevitable for there to be friction in any kind of connection. It is crucial to acquire the skills necessary to resolve disagreements constructively. Instead of laying blame, you should concentrate on finding solutions, and you should be prepared to apologize when it is required.

Social Awareness

It is essential to have a solid grasp of social dynamics and protocol to successfully navigate a variety of social settings. It is important to be aware of social cues, to respect personal boundaries, and to be aware of cultural differences.

Self-Confidence

The ability to connect with people and have faith in your capacity to do so is essential to expanding your social circle. Have faith in your value as a friend, and approach new social settings with confidence in what you have to offer.

Positivity

Your connections with your pals might benefit from you keeping a happy attitude and giving them your unconditional support. The cultivation of a positive attitude within your social group may provide an upbeat and pleasurable environment.

Making New Friends

The process of making new acquaintances may be quite thrilling, but it can also be rather difficult at times. The following are some methods that will assist you in broadening your social circle and establishing new connections:

Pursue Your Interests

Participate in pursuits and pastimes that pique your interest. It will be simpler for you to build relationships with like-minded people since the likelihood of meeting others who share your hobbies will be higher.

Be Approachable

Being friendly and approachable is an appealing attribute. Keep an open body language, flash a kind smile, and show genuine interest in the people around you. When others feel at ease approaching you, they are more inclined to initiate contact with you.

Initiate Conversations

Take the initiative to establish discussions with individuals whose company you would want to enjoy more so that you may learn more about them. Start by offering simple pleasantries, and then gradually create rapport with the other person by asking questions and demonstrating genuine interest in what they have to say.

Be a Good Listener

A beneficial ability in social interaction is careful listening. Not only do you make the other person feel heard when you actively listen to them, but you also receive insights into the thoughts and feelings that they are experiencing.

Attend Social Events

Take part in social get-togethers, groups, or activities that are related to the things you're interested in. These kinds of environments make it easy to strike up conversations with new people who have interests similar to your own.

Volunteer

Volunteering for an organization that supports a cause that is important to you can put you in touch with others who share your values and give you the satisfaction of making a positive contribution to the community.

Online Communities

Connecting with others who have similar interests as you may be accomplished through the use of online platforms such as social media and forums, for example. However, keep in mind the importance of practicing safe behavior online and being wary when engaging with unknown people.

Nurturing Friendships

Developing a friendship is only the first step; it is equally as necessary to keep it going strong and give it attention. The following are some ways in which you may maintain healthy connections while still being a good friend:

Stay in Touch

Put up the effort to keep in touch regularly. Maintaining regular contact with one another, whether through phone conversations, messages, or in-person get-togethers, is an important step in keeping the relationship alive.

Show Appreciation

Show your pals how much they mean to you by expressing your thanks and appreciation. A straightforward "thank you" or sincere praise might go a long way toward enhancing the quality of your relationship with another person.

Be Reliable

Trust is built on dependable behavior and actions. Be someone who your friends can rely on by honoring the commitments you make to them and being available for them whenever they want assistance.

Be Supportive

You should encourage your friends in whatever efforts they undertake, celebrate their successes, and be there for them when they are struggling with difficulties. A reliable friend is someone who can always be counted on to offer support and inspiration.

Resolve Conflicts Gracefully

Every friendship can experience disagreements. When they do, respond to them empathically and with a willingness to find a solution that is beneficial to both sides.

Respect Boundaries

Always respect the limits and personal space established by your buddies. Realize that everyone possesses their very own set of boundaries and comfort zones.

Be Understanding

Recognize that others are living their own lives, which are full of their obligations and struggles. Exhibit compassion and understanding when your pals are unable to constantly be there for you.

Friendship in the Digital Age

Friendships may now exist even when people are not close to one another, thanks to the rise of digital technology. Friendships formed via the Internet are becoming increasingly prevalent and may be equally as significant as those formed in person. However, it is essential to strike a good balance between offline and online relationships, and whenever it is feasible to do so, you should place a higher priority on face-to-face connections.

Keep in mind that maintaining friendships, much like maintaining any other connection, takes work and attention. You may form and keep meaningful friendships that contribute to the enrichment of your life if you work on strengthening your social skills and building good habits.

Chapter 7

Communication Skills: The Art of Making Yourself Heard

To communicate with other people, communication is essential. Communication is essential for forming and establishing bonds with others because it allows us to convey our thoughts, feelings, ideas, and intentions. Understanding and being understood by others are equally important components of clear speech. If you want to thrive socially, academically, and beyond as a teenager, you should work on strengthening your communication abilities.

The Importance of Communication

What makes communication so important? Think about these major factors:

Expressing Needs and Desires

Sharing your wants, needs, and emotions with others is facilitated through effective communication. Whether you're venting to a pal about your day or having a serious conversation with your instructor about your future, good communication is key.

Building Relationships

Strong bonds are built on solid communication. It's a great way to build rapport and get closer to someone. Maintaining healthy relationships with those you care about most requires an ability to talk openly and honestly with them.

Conflict Resolution

When disagreements emerge, talking things out is the key to finding a solution. It is possible to resolve conflicts and please everyone concerned via reasonable discussion and compromise.

Academic Success

To excel in school, you need to be able to express yourself clearly. Having strong communication skills will help you succeed in school, whether you're giving oral presentations or leading group discussions.

Career Advancement

Effective communication skills are increasingly important as you enter adulthood. Employers place a high premium on these qualities, and having them can open doors for you professionally.

Elements of Effective Communication

The ability to communicate effectively requires a wide range of abilities, including the following:

Listening

Active listening is the cornerstone of effective dialogue. Understanding someone's message, thoughts, and intentions requires more than just hearing the words they use to express them. Giving someone your undivided attention while also asking questions and offering responses that demonstrate your comprehension is an example of active listening.

Verbal Communication

The words you say or write are both part of verbal communication. Communicating with precision and brevity is crucial. Pick your words wisely, modulate your pace, and adopt an attitude that befits the message you wish to deliver.

Verbal Communication

Facial expressions, body language, and gestures are examples of nonverbal clues that can convey more meaning than words alone. Think about how your message could be received and how your nonverbal cues might affect it.

Empathy

To have empathy is to feel and comprehend what other people are going through. Trying to understand a problem from another person's point of view requires imagining oneself in their shoes. Communicating with empathy demonstrates consideration for the other person's feelings.

Clarity

If you want your message to have the desired effect, you need to communicate it. When communicating verbally or in writing, steer clear of jargon and convoluted vocabulary. If you need to make your point clearer, use examples and analogies.

Respect

Communicating with respect is taking into account the thoughts and feelings of the other person. Don't resort to name-calling or other insults, even if you disagree with someone. Do unto others as you would have them do towards you.

Communication Skills in Practice

We've covered the fundamentals of good communication; now let's get into some specific abilities you may use in your everyday life:

Active Listening

Active listening entails paying complete attention to the speaker. Keep your mouth shut and use phrases like "I see" and "Go on" to demonstrate that you're following along. Restate what you think you heard to check your understanding.

Expressing Yourself

Always aim for clarity and brevity when expressing yourself. Avoid accusation and blame by expressing your opinion using "I" phrases. Rather than "You never listen to me," try "I feel unheard when..."

Nonverbal Awareness

Watch your body language and read the nuances. Keep your body language open and inviting, and watch your emotions and tone of voice. It's important to coordinate your vocal and nonverbal messages.

Empathetic Responses

Gain experience in empathy by learning to recognize and respect the emotions of others. To comfort a sad buddy, you may say something like, "I can see that you're feeling frustrated about this."

Asking Questions

As well as demonstrating your engagement in the discussion, questions are a great way to learn more about the topic at hand. Conversations with greater depth are fostered by the use of open-ended inquiries.

Conflict Resolution

When disagreements emerge, try to think of ways to resolve them. Take into account the other person's point of view, articulate your own, and negotiate a solution that accommodates your differences.

Pitch and Tone

Watch how high or low you let your voice go. A confident and respectful tone comes out as calm and balanced. Never use a loud voice or an angry tone, no matter how passionate your dispute is.

Feedback

Don't be afraid to give some helpful criticism when it's due. Communicate your thoughts and ideas in a way that is constructive and kind.

Improving Your Communication Skills

Effort and practice are necessary to hone any ability, and communication is no exception. If you want to become a better communicator, try these techniques:

Practice Active Listening

Make an effort to engage in attentive listening in your day-to-day conversations. Focus on the people you're talking to and try to understand what they're saying, whether they're friends, relatives, or teachers.

Join Clubs or Groups

Participate in activities by joining relevant clubs, groups, and societies. You may hone your communication abilities in both professional and casual situations.

Seek Feedback

To improve your communication skills, it's a good idea to get advice from people you trust. They may have some excellent ideas for enhancing the situation.

Read and Write

Vocabulary and expression can be expanded by exposure to print media, whether in the form of books, articles, essays, or diaries. Writing helps you express your views clearly, while reading introduces you to new ideas and writing styles.

Practice Public Speaking

Mastering the art of public speaking may serve you well in a variety of contexts, from giving presentations in class to acing your next job interview. Gain assurance by recording or practicing in front of yourself.

Use Technology Wisely

Although technology facilitates communication, it's important to consider how much time you spend communicating digitally and how it can affect your interpersonal skills. Maintain a mix of virtual and real-world connections.

Communication in the Digital Age

Now that we live in a digital age, there are many more ways to get in touch with one another than ever before. Despite the benefits, it is always important to be polite and kind while communicating online.

Keep in mind that the same rules of good communication also apply while interacting with others online:

- Be clear and concise in your written messages.
- Use a respectful tone and avoid online conflicts.
- Consider the impact of your words and the potential for misunderstandings.
- Practice digital etiquette and respect others' boundaries and privacy.

Chapter 8

Relationship Skills: Managing Love and Friendships

Companions, support, and a feeling of belonging are just some of the things we get out of our relationships with other people. You are at an age where you are learning how to navigate friendships and love relationships. Achieving and maintaining meaningful relationships calls for the cultivation of healthy interpersonal skills.

The Complexity of Relationships

There are a wide variety of relationships, each with its own set of advantages and disadvantages. As an adolescent, you could experience the following relationships:

Friendships

You can't have a stable social life without good friends. Friends provide company, emotional support, and new perspectives. Communication, trust, and mutual regard are the building blocks of a healthy friendship.

Family Relationships

The bonds you share with your parents, siblings, and other relatives shape who you are and how you approach the world. These connections have the potential to bring you joy and solace, but they also carry the risk of bringing out the worst in you.

Romantic Relationships

Adolescence is a time when many people first experience romantic attraction and start dating seriously for the first time.

These connections may be thrilling and rewarding, but they also call for open dialogue, trust, and emotional maturity on both sides.

Peer Relationships

You can't grow as a person socially and emotionally in isolation from your classmates and friends. Peer groups have a significant impact on individuals' sense of self-worth, values, and actions.

Mentorships

A mentor is someone who helps you develop personally and professionally by sharing their knowledge and experience with you. These connections are a rich source of information and instruction.

Online Relationships

Online communities, games, and social networks have all contributed to the rise in popularity of interacting with others online. Although they facilitate communication, using them securely and ethically is a must.

Building Healthy Relationships

When two people have these qualities in their relationships, they can work together and support one another. If you're looking to make new friends or strengthen the bonds with the ones you already have, consider these guidelines.

Communication

The cornerstone of any happy relationship is open and honest dialogue. Communicate your ideas, emotions, and wants plainly, and show genuine interest in the other person's point of view.

Trust

The foundation of any successful relationship is trust. It takes time and regular effort to build trust. Establish trust with others by always coming through on your promises.

Boundaries

To keep relationships from becoming toxic, it is crucial to set and uphold appropriate limits. Relationship boundaries outline the types of conduct that are and are not tolerated by those involved.

Empathy

By putting yourself in another person's shoes, or developing empathy, you can form stronger bonds with those around you. Recognize their feelings and be there for them when they need you.

Conflict Resolution

Inevitably, there will be fights in your relationship. Active listening, compromising, and a commitment to finding solutions that work for all parties are all part of learning how to handle disagreements constructively.

Respect

It's crucial to honor the other person's right to their thoughts and experiences. Even if you disagree with someone, you should treat them with love and respect.

Support

Provide comfort and solace to those close to you. Be supportive, helpful, and appreciative of their accomplishments.

Friendships: Quality Over Quantity

As an adolescent, you can feel that you need to prove your popularity by belonging to a popular organization or having a huge buddy circle. The quality, rather than the quantity, of your friendships is what counts. Here are some traits shared by genuine friends:

Trustworthiness

Real friends can always be counted on in a time of need. They are reliable because they follow through on what they say they will do.

Loyalty

True friends stick by you through the good times and the bad. They have your back and will always be there for you, no matter what.

Acceptance

Friends are those who love you despite your imperfections. They don't attempt to mold you into something you're not.

Supportive

Friends who are available to listen, give advice when requested, and lend emotional support are invaluable. They have your best interests at heart.

Respectful

Mutual regard is the cornerstone of a strong friendship. Real friends will never cross your limits or question your choices.

Fun and Laughter

Relationships with friends need to be satisfying and fulfilling. True friends brighten your life with joy and laughter.

Romantic Relationships: Navigating the Journey

It's important to take things slowly and thoughtfully while you explore romantic possibilities. Some essential considerations include:

Self-Awareness

Learn who you are, what you value, and where you want to go in life before being involved with someone romantically. It's important to be clear on your relationship priorities.

Communication

In a love connection, it is much more important to communicate well. Talk openly and honestly about what you want, what your limits are, and your worries.

Consent

All strong romantic relationships are built on a firm basis of mutual consent. Any kind of physical or intimate interaction requires the full and passionate participation of both participants.

Mutual Respect

Each person's right to their thoughts, feelings, and space must be respected. Mutual respect is the cornerstone of a happy love relationship.

Emotional Health

Keep your emotional health in check while in a committed relationship. If you're having trouble, it's fine to talk to someone for help.

Growth

Personal development and progress are aided by maintaining positive relationships. Boost one another's aims and ambitions.

Healthy Boundaries

Boundaries in a love relationship should be healthy and mutually respected. Having clear boundaries in place might make both people feel more secure.

Navigating Challenges

There are always going to be difficulties in a partnership. When things get challenging, it's important to keep in mind that it's natural to go through highs and lows. Challenges in interpersonal connections can be navigated with the following strategies:

Open Communication

Have a conversation with the other individual about your worries and how you're feeling. It is possible to confront problems and locate solutions with the aid of honest communication.

Seek Guidance

If you are experiencing difficult challenges in a relationship, it may be beneficial to seek advice from a trusted friend, a member of your family, or a professional counselor.

Self-Care

Take care of your mental and emotional health. Your well-being depends on it. Make it a top priority to engage in activities that promote self-care and help you rest and refresh.

Patience

Growing and developing a relationship takes time and patience on both parties' parts. While you are working through difficulties, use patience with both yourself and the other person.

Learn from Experiences

Consider the difficulties that arise in relationships to be learning and development opportunities. Think about what you've picked up from this experience and how you can apply it to make your future relationships better.

Ending Unhealthy Relationships

Recognizing and addressing harmful or poisonous relationships is just as important as developing healthy ones. Manipulation, control, contempt, and emotional or physical abuse are all red flags for an unhealthy relationship. Here are some things to do if you're in an unhealthy relationship:

Recognize the Signs

Learn the warning signs of a toxic relationship. Having an understanding of the problem is the first step towards solving it.

Seek Support

Get help from people you trust, whether they be friends, family, or professionals. You can get help if you're in a toxic relationship.

Set Boundaries

A good relationship requires both parties to set limits and share their expectations for the partnership. It may be time to leave the relationship if the other person cannot respect your limits.

Prioritize Your Well-Being

Take care of yourself first and foremost. It's crucial to safeguard oneself if a romantic connection is causing bodily or mental pain.

End the Relationship

Be ready to cut the cord if you find yourself in an unhealthy relationship. Although it may be difficult, this option may be necessary to ensure your safety and well-being.

Chapter 9

Respect and Equality: Understanding Gender Roles and Responsibilities

Understanding and fostering respect and equality are essential concepts for maintaining good relationships and a healthy society as a whole in a world that is home to a wide variety of cultures, ethnicities, and identities. Teenagers are in a special position to learn about and accept the ideas of gender roles and duties. Doing so may have a substantial impact on both their relationships with other people and their comprehension of the world around them.

What Are Gender Roles and Responsibilities?

Gender roles are the cultural expectations and standards that determine how persons of various genders should act, how they should express themselves, and how they should carry out particular responsibilities in society. These roles might vary from culture to culture and from historical era to historical period, but they typically include stereotypical depictions of what constitutes "appropriate" conduct for men, women, and persons who identify with genders other than male and female.

On the other side, gender responsibilities refer to the tasks, duties, and obligations that individuals are expected to accomplish depending on their gender. These expectations vary from culture to culture. These obligations can range from more conventional tasks such as providing care and assistance to more contemporary activities such as obtaining a profession or being involved in political action.

43

The Impact of Gender Roles

It is important to get an understanding of gender roles and to critically examine them since they have the potential to impact many facets of your life, including the following:

Relationships

Expectations in love engagements, friendships, and the dynamics of families can be influenced by traditional gender roles. For instance, the notion that males should be stoic and unemotional might make it more difficult for couples to have open conversations about their feelings.

Career Choices

There is a correlation between gender roles and employment options. Because some occupations have traditionally been linked with particular genders, this has the potential to restrict possibilities and maintain inequality in the workplace.

Self-Identity

Furthermore, gender roles can affect how an individual views themselves concerning their place in society. To achieve a higher sense of self-awareness and authenticity, it is helpful to question and challenge these positions.

Social Norms

Through the use of societal norms and expectations, society frequently acts to reinforce gender roles. By gaining an understanding of these standards, you may better handle the demands that are placed on you by society and make more informed decisions.

Breaking Down Gender Stereotypes

Gender stereotypes are fixed views about how people of various sexes are "supposed to be" in terms of their appearance, personality, and behavior. Harmful preconceptions like these can help keep prejudice, discrimination, and injustice at bay. Some typical gender roles are as follows:

1. Women are Emotionally Expressive; Men are Stoic

This generalization assumes that men are emotionally numb and expressionless, whereas women are predisposed to feel and show more emotion. It's beneficial to express the whole spectrum of emotions that we all feel, regardless of our gender.

2. Men are Breadwinners; Women are Caregivers

Men are seen as the breadwinners in this stereotype, while women are seen as the primary carers and homemakers. However, men and women can choose to either work or care for others or do both.

3. Men are Aggressive; Women are Passive

According to this generalization, males are more likely to act aggressively and dominantly than women. Assumptions like this can fuel unhealthy power relations and disagreements.

4. Gender and Interests

Gender stereotypes regarding interests and hobbies are pervasive in today's culture. Some people may think that guys should do sports and girls should stay in the kitchen. In truth, people of both sexes should have equal opportunities to pursue their passions.

The Importance of Gender Equality

The concept and practice of gender equality are based on the idea that people of both sexes should be afforded the same respect and opportunity as those of the other. Advancing gender parity is good for society as a whole because it makes it more equitable and welcoming. Reasons why gender equality is important include the following:

Human Rights

There should be no discrimination based on a person's gender. Everyone, regardless of their gender, should be afforded the same rights and privileges and treated with respect and decency.

Social Justice

The pursuit of social justice requires the promotion of gender parity. It's a tool in the fight against bigotry and false beliefs that contribute to a cycle of disadvantage.

Economic Benefits

Equal pay for equal work benefits the economy. Individuals' productivity and creativity improve when they are not hindered by stereotypes based on their gender in the workplace.

Mental and Emotional Well-Being

The mental and emotional health of a population benefits from gender parity. When people are not expected to conform to stereotypical gender norms, they are more likely to develop their full potential.

Healthy Relationships

Relationships benefit from the promotion of gender equality because they are healthier and fairer. It promotes honest expression, tolerance for differences, and solidarity in all kinds of interactions.

Challenging Gender Roles and Responsibilities

Respect and equality may be advanced through challenging established gender roles and duties. You may help by doing the following things:

Self-Reflection

To get started, think about how you feel about gender. Think about how your exposure to various forms of media and culture may have influenced your worldview.

Educate Yourself

Read about the struggles of people throughout history who have questioned traditional gender roles. Books, films, and the internet all have their place as educational materials.

Support Gender Equality Initiatives

Help groups and causes that are challenging harmful gender conventions and working toward gender equality. You may make a significant impact with your participation.

Be a Role Model

Set a good example. Do things that go against the grain of socially accepted gender norms, whether it's pursuing your passions, helping out around the house, or standing up for your loved ones' decisions.

Encourage Conversations

Start discussions on expected and preferred gender behaviors and duties among your social circle. Initiate debates where people may share their ideas without fear of reprisal.

Chapter 10

Shared Household Responsibilities: Why Everyone Should Pitch In

Collaboration and the division of domestic chores are the cornerstones of a peaceful home. The concept of shared duties is becoming increasingly prevalent in today's society, which is leading to a shift away from conventional gender roles within homes. You, as a teen, have the chance to learn about and participate in this significant transformation, which will ensure that everyone in your home plays a role in keeping your living environment clean and orderly.

The Evolution of Household Responsibilities

When it comes to the tasks of running a home, many different civilizations in the past strictly adhered to gender norms. Women were traditionally expected to carry out the bulk of household responsibilities, such as cooking, cleaning, and caring for children, while men were largely responsible for providing for the family financially.

On the other hand, the norms of society have changed, and today's homes are growing more varied and egalitarian. Many households in today's society understand the significance of equally dividing household tasks and working together to take care of the house. This change is beneficial to all parties involved since it encourages justice, lessens the strain on any one person, and helps to develop a sense of togetherness within the family.

The Benefits of Shared Household Responsibilities

The benefits of shared home chores extend to individuals as well as families, and include the following:

Equality

By subverting the conventional gender norms and expectations that have been placed on individuals, shared responsibilities contribute to the advancement of gender equality. Everyone in the family, regardless of gender, is appreciated for the roles that they play in the household.

Reduced Stress

When everyone in the family contributes to the completion of their assigned tasks, the burden of labor is reduced. Because of this, one may experience less stress and a calmer atmosphere in their daily lives.

Life Skills

Teenagers and young adults can benefit from participating in domestic activities, as it helps them learn key life skills such as cooking, cleaning, and managing their time effectively.

Teamwork

A spirit of collaboration and cooperation may flourish within a family when tasks are divided and shared. The relationships that hold a family together can be strengthened by working together toward similar goals.

Independence

Those adolescents and young adults who are actively involved in the management of home tasks develop the skills necessary for independence and self-sufficiency, which in turn prepares them for adulthood.

Learning Empathy

Members of the family who take on duties are better able to empathize with and understand one another because they have a better knowledge of the problems and strengths faced by one another.

Identifying Household Tasks

Identifying the many home duties that need attention is crucial for successfully implementing shared responsibility. There are a few main types of housework:

Cooking and Meal Preparation

Meal preparation encompasses menu planning, food buying, preparation, and cleanup. The whole family may bond while learning new skills by working together in the kitchen.

Cleaning and Organization

Keeping one's home clean and organized is a part of daily life. Cleaning duties might include sweeping, mopping, dusting, doing laundry, and arranging communal spaces.

Yard Work

Lawn care, gardening, and general outside tidying are all part of yard chores. Pet care and the maintenance of external areas like balconies and porches still count as outdoor obligations even if you don't have a yard.

Childcare

Childcare entails monitoring and meeting the needs of young children belonging to working households. When it comes to taking care of younger siblings, older siblings may be a huge help.

Financial Management

Budgeting, bill paying, and keeping tabs on costs might all fall under the scope of one's financial obligations. Teenagers can gain valuable experience in money management by participating in these activities, even though they are more suited to adults.

Maintenance and Repairs

Changing light bulbs, making small repairs, and checking the functionality of equipment are all part of house maintenance. The household as a whole benefits from learning some preventative maintenance skills.

Creating a Household Responsibility Plan

The following are some suggestions for achieving successful shared responsibility implementation:

Family Discussion

Start a conversation with your loved ones about the advantages of taking on joint tasks. Getting to know each member of the family requires an open dialogue and attentive listening.

Task Assignment

Make a list of chores that need doing around the house, then divide them up according to who can do what best. Keep an open mind and be prepared to make changes to your tasks.

Schedule

Make doing chores around the house part of your routine. This can make it easier to delegate tasks and communicate expectations throughout the team.

Support and Encouragement

Give loved ones your full backing when they take on new challenges. Recognize and honor their efforts and successes.

Review and Adjust

The success of the plan to teach home responsibility should be evaluated regularly. Make any required changes to guarantee a balanced and fair distribution of labor.

Tips for Teenagers

When it comes to domestic chores, you as a teenager may have some unique concerns:

Time Management

It can be difficult to juggle academics, extracurriculars, and chores. Mastering time management techniques can help you keep your word.

Independence

Taking on more responsibility around the house is a great way to show that you can work independently and have a positive impact on your family's life. Accept these obligations as challenges that will push you to develop as a person.

Communicate

If you're having trouble keeping everything in balance, talk to your loved ones about how you're feeling. When people talk to one another honestly and openly, they may find solutions that benefit everyone.

Learn Life Skills

Learning to manage a household properly equips you with skills that will serve you well in later life. Accept the necessity of continuous education and the growth of your abilities.

Chapter 11

Respect for Women: The Importance of Consent and Boundaries

Understanding the value of permission and setting appropriate limits is crucial to maintaining positive relationships and growing as an individual. You, as a teenager, have a pivotal role in spreading these values and creating an atmosphere based on mutual regard and fair treatment.

The Foundations of Respect

No matter the gender of the people involved, respect must always be present. Respecting people entails listening to them, considering what they have to say, and recognizing their right to make their own decisions. Here are some important guidelines to follow while thinking about how to treat women with respect:

Equality

To show respect for women, one must first acknowledge their inherent value and liberties. There should be no difference in value or opportunity based on a person's gender.

Consent

A person's permission is required before engaging in any kind of physical contact, whether it's with a friend, a love partner, or anybody else. All persons participating in an action or behavior provide their consent when they do it voluntarily. It ought to be well thought out, full of energy, and continuing.

Boundaries

When you respect someone's boundaries, you take into account and value their personal space and limitations. It is important to recognize and discuss personal limits in all relationships.

Empathy

The capacity for empathy is defined as the awareness and acceptance of another's emotional state. One way to strengthen your relationships with women is to work on developing your capacity for empathy.

Active Listening

To actively listen means to pay attention to what another person is saying without interrupting or passing judgment. It shows that you value their opinion and input.

The Importance of Consent

Respecting women and encouraging positive relationships requires an emphasis on consent. It's not just the right thing to do, but often the lawful thing to do as well. Some fundamentals of the concept of consent are as follows:

Informed Consent

All parties to a consent agreement must have full knowledge of the terms before giving their approval. Knowing the inherent dangers and having the freedom to alter one's opinion at any moment are all part of this.

Enthusiastic Consent

A positive and passionate response is required for consent. An unqualified "yes" is preferable to the silence of a "no." Any hesitancy or vagueness in a person's response indicates a lack of permission.

Ongoing Consent

The act of giving one's consent is ongoing. Constantly reassess your partner's level of comfort and willingness to go forward to make sure everyone is on the same page. Consent is voluntary and must be honored if revoked at any time.

Alcohol and Drugs

A person's ability to offer informed consent is compromised by the effects of alcohol and other substances. Sexual action without the other person's permission is always wrong.

Consent Is Not Assumed

No one should ever be presumed to have given their permission based on their outward look or behavior. For every encounter, it must be knowingly and willingly provided.

Communicating Boundaries

Promoting respect for women also involves recognizing and honoring personal space. It's important to talk about and respect each other's limits. Methods for Dealing with Limits

Open Communication

It's important to promote honest and open dialogue with the ladies in your life. Inquire into their comfort zones and share your own, if you feel comfortable doing so.

Respect Their Decisions

If a lady expresses her want for space, you should give her that space without questioning or pressuring her. Respecting someone else's boundaries shows respect for them.

Check-In Regularly

It's important for people in committed relationships to constantly assess whether or not their boundaries are being upheld.

Consent and Boundaries Go Hand-in-Hand

There is a connection between limits and consent. Consent refers to a person's willingness to take part in an activity, whereas boundaries indicate the limits to which that person is willing to go.

Boundaries Are Empowering

Individuals gain agency in their relationships and experiences

when their boundaries are respected. Everyone will feel more secure and at ease as a result.

Promoting Respect for Women

You may actively encourage respect for women in the way that you live your life and interact with others even as a teenager. The following are some useful actions that you can take:

Educate Yourself

Educate yourself about the concepts of permission and limits, as well as the significance of respect in interpersonal interactions. Acquiring knowledge is the first step in advancing the cause of these ideas.

Lead by Example

Establish an example of respectful conduct in your relationships with women as well as in your interactions with other people. Your deeds have the potential to affect the people around you.

Challenge Harmful Norms

Raise your voice in protest against damaging assumptions, attitudes, or actions that objectify or degrade women and speak out against them. In talks and other social situations, you should try to challenge these standards.

Support Survivors

If someone confides in you that they have been subjected to any type of harassment or abuse, it is your responsibility to provide support, empathy, and encouragement to seek the assistance of a professional, if necessary.

Be an Active Bystander

If you see someone acting disrespectfully or crossing a boundary, you should step in and correct the situation whenever it is safe and acceptable to do so. Your participation has the potential to make a huge impact.

Chapter 12

Handling Peer Pressure: On Substance Abuse and Alcohol

During the teenage years, one of the most prevalent and significant influences is that of one's peers. It is a phase in a person's life when they frequently seek acceptance and approval from their contemporaries. Even though there are some positive aspects to peer pressure, it may become a problem when it encourages potentially harmful actions such as abusing substances or drinking an excessive amount of alcohol. In this chapter, we will discuss the mechanics of peer pressure, its influence, as well as effective ways of dealing with it while still choosing decisions that are safe and appropriate.

Understanding Peer Pressure

The influence that is exerted by a peer group on people, urging them to modify their attitudes, actions, or values to adhere to the standards or expectations of the group, is referred to as peer pressure. It may present itself in a variety of ways, including the following:

Direct Pressure

When other people, often your peers, make it clear that they want you to engage in a certain activity or put pressure on you to do so, such as taking drugs or alcohol.

Indirect Pressure

The influence that comes from seeing other people in your peer group participating in specific activities, might lead to you feeling forced to do the same things yourself.

Social Pressure

If you want to be a part of your peer group and have them, accept you, you may end up conforming to the expectations that they have for you, even if you disagree with certain behaviors.

Self-Imposed Pressure

Individuals could put pressure on themselves to adhere to the standards of their peer group because they are afraid of being left out or laughed at if they don't behave expectedly.

The Impact of Peer Pressure

Individuals are susceptible to both positive and negative outcomes as a result of the influence of their peers. Good activities can be encouraged by positive peer pressure, such as continuing one's education, participating in sports, or volunteering in the community. On the other hand, negative peer pressure frequently results in bad outcomes, especially when it comes to the usage of substances and alcohol. Teenagers can be negatively affected in the following ways by negative peer pressure:

Risky Behaviors

Teenagers who are subjected to unfavorable peer pressure may engage in dangerous activities, such as experimenting with drugs, alcohol, or other potentially harmful substances.

Health Consequences

Abuse of substances and excessive consumption of alcohol may have serious negative effects on both a person's physical and mental health, including but not limited to addiction, accidents, and mental health issues.

Academic and Personal Life

The consequences of being subjected to unhealthy levels of peer pressure can extend into all aspects of a person's life, including their academic achievement, their relationships, and even their legal problems.

Emotional Toll

Emotional pain, feelings of guilt, and a reduction in one's self-esteem can be the end consequence of feeling compelled to adhere to undesirable habits.

Long-Term Consequences

Peer pressure can lead someone to engage in dangerous activities, which can have long-term repercussions, including an impact on future educational and professional chances.

Strategies for Handling Peer Pressure

It takes a mix of self-awareness, assertiveness, and the ability to make decisions well to effectively handle the pressure that comes from peers. The following are some methods that can assist you in making responsible and secure decisions:

Self-Reflection

Spend some time thinking about what you believe, what your values are, and where your limits lay. When you are well aware of the values you uphold, it is much simpler to withstand pressure that runs counter to those values.

Choose Your Friends Wisely

Put yourself in an environment where you are surrounded by people who share your beliefs and will support the decisions you make to be responsible.

Practice Assertiveness

Acquire the skill of expressing your thoughts and emotions confidently. When confronted with the pressure to participate in harmful activities, work on expressing "no" in a manner that is forceful yet polite.

Plan Ahead

Prepare yourself for circumstances where you may be subjected to the influence of your peers, such as parties or other social events. Prepare a strategy for how you will react and have it handy.

Develop Refusal Skills

Develop your ability to refuse so that you may politely but firmly turn down offers or invitations to participate in risky behaviors. To bolster your self-assurance, try acting out different scenarios with a reliable friend or member of your family.

Be Informed

Get yourself informed on the dangers and outcomes associated with alcohol and drug misuse. Your determination to ignore the influence of your peers can be strengthened by having a better understanding of the potential risks.

Seek Support

Discuss the issue of the pressure from your peers with an adult who you can put your faith in, such as a parent, guardian, teacher, or counselor. They can offer direction and assistance.

Find Alternatives

Find other ways to spend your time and join social groups that are in line with your principles and passions. Participating in healthy, productive activities might help lessen one's vulnerability to destructive forms of peer pressure.

Practice Peer Pressure Resistance

Putting up a fight against the pressures of your peers requires practice and the support of those who share your ideals. Build a support system of peers who can encourage and guide one another to make decisions that are in their best interests.

Understand Consequences

Think about the probable repercussions of caving into the pressure of your peers. Think about how it could affect your health, the connections you have, and your plans for the future.

Know When to Walk Away

If you find yourself in a circumstance in which the pressure from your peers is excessive, do not be afraid to withdraw yourself from the situation. Your health and safety should always come before everything else.

Part IV

Physical and Mental Well-Being

Chapter 13

Health and Nutrition: Fueling Your Body and Mind

Your mental and physical health are intimately connected to the foods you consume and how you provide nourishment for your body. Because you are going through a period of fast physical development and growth, you must be aware of the significance of maintaining a healthy diet at this time. This chapter examines the principles of health and nutrition and gives practical information for making educated food choices that will support your body and mind. The focus of this chapter is on preventing and managing chronic diseases.

The Connection Between Nutrition and Health

The way you eat is one of the most important factors in determining your overall health. It supplies the critical nutrients that your body needs to develop and heal itself, as well as function at its highest possible level. A healthy diet not only plays a role in the maintenance of your physical health but also plays a key role in the maintenance of your mental well-being. The following is a list of important factors about this connection:

Physical Health

Nutrition affects every facet of a person's physical health, from the solidity of their bones and muscles to the performance of their internal organs and systems. A healthy development, immunological function, and energy level are all supported by a well-balanced diet.

Mental Health

For it to operate properly, your brain requires particular nutrients. Inadequate nutrition can result in irritability, exhaustion, and even mental health conditions such as sadness and anxiety.

Energy Levels

The majority of the energy that your body needs comes from the food that you consume. Your ability to maintain an active and engaged lifestyle throughout your day is directly correlated to the quality of the nutrition you consume.

Immune System

The health of your immune system is directly influenced by the nutrition that you consume. When it comes to fighting off diseases and infections, a body that is properly fed has an advantage.

The Basics of a Healthy Diet

A healthy diet includes a wide range of foods, all of which include the critical elements that your body needs. Carbohydrates, proteins, lipids, vitamins, minerals, and water are all included in this category of nutrients. An explanation of each component is as follows:

Carbohydrates

The major source of fuel for the body is comprised of carbohydrates. carbs may be broken down into two categories: simple carbs, which can be found in sweet meals and beverages, and complex carbohydrates, which can be found in whole grains, fruits, vegetables, and legumes. Choose complex carbs if you want your energy to last longer.

Proteins

Proteins are necessary for the development, maintenance, and repair of tissues, and the manufacturing of enzymes and hormones.

Lean cuts of meat, chicken, fish, eggs, and dairy products, as well as nuts and legumes, are all excellent sources of protein.

Fats

Consuming fats in the right amounts, however, is essential for good health but moderation is key. Avocados, nuts, seeds, and fatty fish like salmon are all good sources of healthy fats, which help maintain healthy skin and cognitive function. Nuts and seeds are also good sources of healthy fats.

Vitamins and Minerals

Vitamins and minerals are required for a wide variety of biological processes, including the maintenance of strong bones and the production of usable energy from the food we eat. You can obtain them by eating fruits, vegetables, whole cereals, and dairy products.

Water

Water is essential for maintaining proper hydration and making sure that all of the functions in your body work efficiently. To ensure that you remain well hydrated throughout the day, make it a priority to consume a lot of water.

The Importance of Balance

Consuming a wide range of foods from each of the different food categories in the appropriate amounts is the hallmark of a diet that is considered to be balanced. It is essential to maintain a healthy diet that does not include excessive amounts of any one vitamin or food type. The following are some suggestions that might help you strike a balance in your diet:

Eat a Rainbow

Consume a wide selection of vibrantly colored fruits and vegetables to guarantee that you are getting a comprehensive spectrum of the vitamins and minerals your body needs.

Portion Control

Take into consideration the size of your servings. Even if you consume nutritious food, consuming too much of it might cause you to gain weight and contribute to other health problems.

Limit Sugary and Processed Foods

Reduce as much as you can the number of sugary snacks, processed meals, and drinks that are rich in added sugars that you consume. These can cause peaks and valleys in one's energy levels.

Healthy Snacking

Instead of grabbing chips or candy, choose nutritious snacks such as fruits, veggies, yogurt, or almonds.

Special Dietary Considerations

Due to food allergies, intolerances, or personal convictions (such as vegetarianism or veganism), certain adolescents may have particular dietary requirements or limits. It's critical to work around these preferences without compromising on nutritional intake. For help figuring out how to incorporate these foods into your diet, talk to your doctor or a qualified dietitian.

Developing Healthy Eating Habits

Healthy eating habits, in addition to knowledge of nutrition fundamentals, are essential for long-term wellness. How to develop and keep a balanced perspective on eating is discussed.

Eat Mindfully

Be mindful of your food and enjoy it to the fullest. Don't eat in front of the television or while otherwise distracted.

Avoid Emotional Eating

Never turn to food to alleviate negative feelings like frustration, loneliness, or boredom. Try other methods of dealing with your emotions, such as working out, chatting with a friend, or learning to relax.

Practice Portion Control

Reduce your portion sizes by using smaller dishes and cutlery. Pay attention to signs of hunger and satiety.

Cook at Home

When you prepare meals at home, you can regulate what goes into them and how they're prepared, making it simpler to prepare well-rounded and nutritious meals.

Stay Hydrated

Take frequent sips from a water bottle. Feelings of hunger are often misinterpretations of thirst.

Avoid Crash Diets

If you're trying to lose weight quickly, stay away from restrictive diets. These diets are risky and usually can't be maintained for long.

Chapter 14

The Teenage Body: Understanding Puberty

Every adolescent goes through puberty, a time of profound change and, at times, difficulty. It's a time of transition from childhood to maturity, marked by physiological, emotional, and mental shifts. Knowing what to expect at this time is crucial for a positive and successful transition into adulthood. In this chapter, we'll delve into the complexities of puberty, from the physical to the emotional, and offer advice on how to accept and thrive during this normal process.

What Is Puberty?

Puberty is a normal and progressive rite of passage from adolescence into adulthood. Although the actual onset age varies from person to person, it usually occurs between the ages of 8 and 13 for females and 9 and 14 for boys. Hormonal shifts commence puberty and set in action a wide range of changes in appearance, behavior, and psychology.

Physical Changes During Puberty

Physical changes occur gradually over several years throughout puberty. These shifts are a natural and necessary part of maturing, even though they might feel overwhelming at the moment. Some of the most noticeable bodily changes that occur throughout puberty are as follows:

Growth Spurt

Rapid development in height, known as a growth spurt, is one of the most obvious changes that occurs throughout puberty.

Hormonal signals drive the body's growth plates (seen at the ends of bones) to expand. The growth spurt normally occurs between the ages of 9 and 15 for girls, and 11 and 17 for boys. Both the duration and the pace of expansion are flexible.

Development of Secondary Sexual Characteristics

The secondary sexual features that define men and females alter dramatically during adolescence. Breast and pubic hair growth are also part of these transitions for females. The development of facial hair, a lower vocal pitch, and bulking up are all secondary sexual traits in boys.

Genital Development

Puberty is characterized by profound alterations to the genitalia. The onset of puberty coincides with the onset of menstruation and the maturation of the uterus in females. The testes enlarge and sperm production begins in young males.

Acne

Acne is only one of the skin changes that can occur as a result of the hormonal shifts that occur throughout puberty. Acne can be controlled with good skincare, but it's important to avoid harsh treatments that might harm the skin.

Body Hair

During puberty, hair grows on both boys' and girls' bodies. Facial, chest and back hair tend to grow more prominently in boys, whereas pubic and underarm hair do so in girls.

Body Odor

Body odor is a common problem throughout puberty because of the increased perspiration. Maintaining control can be aided by proper hygiene practices including frequent bathing and the use of deodorant.

Weight Gain

Due to changes in body composition, it is usual for adolescents to gain weight throughout puberty. This sort of weight increase is a natural and healthy component of development.

Emotional and Psychological Changes

Puberty not only causes physical changes but also emotional and mental shifts. These shifts can be equally as profound and difficult to handle. Some of the mental and emotional changes that occur throughout puberty are as follows:

Mood Swings

Teenagers' fluctuating hormone levels might cause them to experience a range of feelings from elation to irritability to depression. Mood swings are normal and to be expected at this time of hormonal transition in the body.

Identity and Self-Discovery

During puberty, adolescents frequently struggle with issues of self-awareness and self-identity. It's a period when you can start to figure out what you care about and what you believe in.

Peer Relationships

Peer networks frequently shift as adolescents enter puberty. Relationships change throughout time, and you may wish to expand your social sphere. It's possible for feelings of peer pressure and the need to fit in to intensify.

Increased Independence

Your desire for freedom from your parents or guardians may increase as you become older. It's a normal aspect of maturing into independence, yet it might cause tension at times.

Sexual Awareness

At puberty, a person's sexual awareness and interest naturally rise. To make educated decisions regarding one's sexual health, thorough and accurate sex education is crucial.

Coping with Puberty

The physical, emotional, and mental shifts that accompany puberty can be difficult to manage, but there are tools available to help you get through it:

Open Communication

Share your thoughts and feelings with an adult you trust, such as a parent, guardian, or school counselor. During this time of change, they may be a reliable source of advice and encouragement.

Educate Yourself

Examine the mental and bodily shifts you're experiencing. Puberty might be less mysterious if you know the science behind it.

Self-Care

Take care of yourself by getting adequate sleep, eating healthy food, and exercising regularly. Take good care of yourself physically and mentally when you enter puberty.

Embrace Your Identity

Examine the things you care about and the ideas you have. Take advantage of the chance to learn about yourself and grow into the person you want to be.

Seek Peer Support

Talk to those who understand what you're going through. Having someone to talk to about what you've been through might help you feel less alone.

Address Emotional Well-Being

Feel free to consult a mental health professional or a counselor if your mood swings or emotional issues become too much to handle on your own. They may offer advice on how to deal with difficult feelings and pressure.

Sex Education

Get educated on all aspects of sexuality from reputable sources. During puberty, it's crucial to gain knowledge about sexuality and how to maintain healthy relationships.

Chapter 15

Mental Health Matters: Taking Care of Your Mind

Your mental health is an integral part of your whole wellness. Prioritizing your mental health is just as important as prioritizing your physical health when it comes to things like nutrition and exercise. Your mental health may be affected by the many changes and difficulties you face during adolescence. In this chapter, we'll talk about what mental health is, how to see the warning symptoms of mental illness, and what you can do to keep your head on straight and improve it.

What Is Mental Health?

To be in good mental health means to be in good emotional, psychological, and social standing. The way you process stress, make decisions, and interact with others are all impacted by your state of mind. Maintaining a sound mind is crucial for success in school, work, and relationships, as well as for handling the inevitable stresses of adulthood.

Common Mental Health Challenges in Adolescence

Physical and mental development accelerates during adolescence. During this period, it's normal to go through a range of emotional and mental difficulties. Adolescents often struggle with the following mental health issues:

Depression

Depressive symptoms include an inability to find joy in anything and an overwhelming melancholy that won't go away. It may interfere with your ability to sleep, to eat, and to feel energetic.

Anxiety

Anxiety disorders are characterized by excessive and unwarranted levels of anxiety, fear, or uneasiness. Anxiety can manifest itself physically in a variety of ways.

Stress

Extreme stress has negative effects on both the mind and the body. Teens can feel overwhelmed by school work, social interactions, and family issues.

Eating Disorders

Disorders including anorexia, bulimia, and binge eating are characterized by destructive eating habits and preoccupations with one's physical appearance.

Substance Abuse

Substance misuse problems emerge when certain adolescents use drugs or alcohol as a means of coping with mental or emotional strain.

Self-Harm

Cutting and other forms of self-injury are common indicators of psychological distress and the need for help.

Suicidal Thoughts

When a person is having suicidal or self-harming thoughts, they need to get treatment right away.

The Importance of Seeking Help

It's crucial to keep in mind that having mental health issues is not a reflection of your failings. Seeking treatment is a courageous act of self-care and acknowledgment of the universality of mental health problems. The best thing you can do for yourself or a loved one who is experiencing mental health difficulties is to get help from a trusted adult, counselor, therapist, or mental health professional.

Strategies for Maintaining and Enhancing Mental Health

Maintaining good mental health is a continual process that necessitates the development of new and better ways of handling stressful situations. Here are some methods for preserving and improving your mental health:

Build a Support System

Talk to someone you trust who is grown and who can provide you comfort and understanding.

Open Communication

Talk to someone you can trust about your innermost thoughts and feelings. Stress and feelings of isolation can be reduced or eliminated when sentiments are spoken.

Practice Self-Care

Focus on things that help you relax and feel better, including self-care. Meditation, deep breathing exercises, and making time for things you like are all examples of this.

Exercise Regularly

Exercising has beneficial effects on one's state of mind. Exercising regularly has been shown to alleviate stress and lift melancholy and anxiety.

Maintain a Balanced Diet

Mental health can benefit from eating right. Emotional health may be bolstered by eating a varied, balanced diet.

Manage Stress

Master stress-busting methods like deep breathing, visualization, and scheduling more downtime.

Set Realistic Goals

Try not to put undue stress on yourself and aim for reasonable targets instead. Reduce daunting tasks into more manageable chunks.

Seek Professional Help

Don't wait to consult a counselor or mental health expert if you're having serious mental health problems. They'll provide you with individualized advice, treatment, and encouragement.

Stay Informed

Learn about the indications of mental illness and the help that is out there. With education, you can tell when you or a friend may use some assistance.

Limit Screen Time

Feelings of inadequacy and stress can be exacerbated by spending too much time in front of the screen, especially on social media. Limit your time spent in front of screens and make in-person time a priority.

Practice Mindfulness

Mindfulness, the practice of paying attention in a certain way on purpose, has been shown to have positive effects on both anxiety and mental health.

Build Resilience

To be resilient is to recover quickly from hardship. The ability to bounce back from adversity is a talent worth cultivating.

Part V

Practical Life Skills

Chapter 16

10 Essential Life Habits: Building Blocks for Success

Living a life that is both meaningful and rewarding is just as important as reaching lofty targets and amassing money. Developing the skills and character traits that will allow you to face adversity head-on and grab chances is crucial if you want to live a fulfilling and fruitful life. In this chapter, we'll look at 10 practices that are crucial to our development and satisfaction as individuals.

Habit 1: Setting Clear Goals

"Setting goals is the first step in turning the invisible into the visible." - Tony Robbins

Life lacks focus and meaning without clearly defined goals. They inspire you to take action and direct your efforts toward the things that matter most. Steps to establishing concise objectives:

Be Specific

Establish clear, quantifiable targets. Rather than just declaring, "I want to get fit," try setting a specific goal such as, "I want to lose 10 pounds in three months."

Make Them Achievable

Goals should be tough but not impossible to achieve. Setting your sights too high might lead to disappointment.

Set Deadlines

Make a plan and set a deadline for yourself to succeed. Setting a deadline instills a sense of panic.

Break Them Down

Break down the large picture into more attainable sub-goals. By doing so, their impact is mitigated.

Write Them Down

Putting your objectives on paper can help you stay focused and monitor your development.

Habit 2: Continuous Learning

"The more that you read, the more things you will know. The more that you learn, the more places you'll go." - Dr. Seuss

Graduation is not the end of your educational journey. Learning is a never-ending process that enriches your life in countless ways. Here's what it takes to commit to lifelong education:

Read Widely

Look into reading material and online content covering a wide range of topics.

Take Courses

To learn something new or to hone your existing abilities, you might choose to enroll in a classroom or online course.

Seek Feedback

Welcoming input from others is a great way to figure out where you can make changes.

Stay Curious

Develop an inquisitive character by constantly questioning things and looking for explanations.

Habit 3: Time Management

"Time is a created thing. To say 'I don't have time' is like saying 'I don't want to." - Lao Tzu

Time management skills are crucial for getting things done and reaching your objectives. It requires setting priorities, avoiding unnecessary interruptions, and making the most of available time. Some suggestions for better time management:

Set Priorities

Prioritize your work by finding the things you need to do the most.

Use Tools

Make good use of planners, lists, and applications that help you manage your time effectively.

Avoid Multitasking

Keep your mind and energy focused on only one thing at a time.

Take Breaks

Taking brief breaks periodically has been shown to increase efficiency.

Habit 4: Financial Literacy

"The lack of money is the root of all evil." - Mark Twain

If you want to be financially secure and independent, you need to learn about money and how to manage it correctly. Educating yourself about money works like this:

Budgeting

Make a plan to record your earnings and expenditures.

Saving

Regularly save aside some of your earnings, no matter how tiny.

Investing

Get educated on your investing choices so that your money can increase over time.

Debt Management

Avoid piling up debt and prioritize paying off any loan with a high-interest rate.

Habit 5: Effective Communication

"The single biggest problem in communication is the illusion that it has taken place." - George Bernard Shaw

Strong relationships, amicable dispute resolution, and fruitful goal attainment all depend on clear and constant communication. How to develop your interpersonal skills:

Active Listening

Listen carefully, ask questions to explain, and try not to interrupt the speaker.

Clear Expression

Communicate your ideas and opinions clearly and briefly.

Empathy

Learn to put yourself in the shoes of others with whom you engage.

Nonverbal Communication

Watch your emotions, gestures, and tone of speech.

Habit 6: Problem-Solving

"The best way to escape from a problem is to solve it." - Alan Saporta

Problems will always be present, but how you deal with them will determine your success. Improve your ability to solve problems via:

Identifying the Problem

Define the problem or difficulty you're trying to solve.

Generating Solutions

Consider all possibilities, no matter how out-of-the-box they may appear.

Evaluating Options

Weigh the benefits of each option against their drawbacks to make a wise decision.

Taking Action

Put your idea into action and keep an eye on how well it's working.

Habit 7: Resilience

"The oak fought the wind and was broken, the willow bent when it must and survived." - Robert Jordan

The ability to recover quickly from setbacks is what we mean when we talk about resilience. The ability to keep going despite obstacles is priceless. Practice resiliency by:

Maintaining a Positive Mindset

Avoid concentrating on difficulties and instead focus on potential answers.

Seeking Support

Whenever you're feeling overwhelmed, it's important to lean on those you care about.

Learning from Setbacks

Try to look at setbacks as educational experiences.

Habit 8: Adaptability

"It is not the strongest of the species that survive, nor the most intelligent, but the one most responsive to change." - Charles Darwin

83

The ability to adjust to changing circumstances and shifts in one's surrounding environment is what we mean when we talk about adaptability. Adaptability is a quality that is extremely useful in a world that is always changing. Create it using means of:

Being Open to Change

Accept change as an opportunity for personal development and advancement.

Learning from Experience

Reflecting on previous experiences to determine what was successful and what was not entails learning from those experiences.

Flexibility

Maintain an open mind to new ways of thinking and doing things.

Habit 9: Healthy Lifestyle

"To keep the body in good health is a duty...otherwise, we shall not be able to keep our minds strong and clear." - Buddha

The mental and physical health of an individual can be improved by adopting a healthy lifestyle. Observe a healthy way of life by doing the following:

Balanced Diet

Consume a wide variety of foods high in nutrients to keep your body and mind fueled.

Regular Exercise

Maintaining physical fitness and relieving stress both need regular exercise.

Adequate Sleep

For the sake of your general well-being, make sure you receive enough quality sleep each night.

Stress Management

Make use of methods that reduce stress such as meditation, yoga, or workouts that include deep breathing.

Habit 10: Social and Emotional Intelligence

"The greatest ability in business is to get along with others and influence their actions." - John Hancock

Understanding and efficiently controlling your own emotions, as well as properly engaging with other people, are both components of social and emotional intelligence. Improve your performance in these areas by:

Self-awareness

Be conscious of your feelings and the influence they have on your actions.

Empathy

Comprehend the experiences and points of view of other people.

Conflict Resolution

Acquire the skills necessary to effectively negotiate conflict.

Relationship Building

Encourage the development of healthy connections with your friends, family, and coworkers.

Chapter 17

Teamwork Skills: Everyone's a Winner

The events of one's life seldom occur in total solitude. At some point or another in our lives, whether it be at school, on the job, or in our personal life, we will find ourselves working with other people. Being a productive member of a team is a valuable ability that not only adds to your success but also the success of the group you're a part of. In this chapter, we will discuss the significance of teamwork, the characteristics of an effective member of a team, as well as methods for enhancing your existing teamwork abilities and cultivating new ones.

The Power of Teamwork

"Individual commitment to a group effort— that is what makes a team work, a company work, a society work, a civilization work." - Vince Lombardi

Individuals coming together to achieve a shared objective is what constitutes teamwork. It makes use of the talents, experiences, and points of view of all of the members of the team to accomplish more than any one person could do on their own. This is why working together in a group is so effective:

Diverse Perspectives

People with a variety of experiences, skill sets, and points of view are brought together to form teams. This variety can lead to creative solutions and decision-making that takes into account all relevant factors.

Shared Responsibility

When people collaborate, they take on a shared responsibility for both the achievements and the failures of the endeavor. This might inspire members of the team to push themselves to achieve their best and to encourage one another.

Efficiency

By delegating responsibilities and capitalizing on the skills of individual team members, groups can finish tasks and projects more quickly.

Learning Opportunities

When you work with other people, you have access to new information and abilities, which is beneficial to your personal growth and development.

Problem-Solving

By tapping on the individual expertise and creative potential of its members, teams may more effectively handle difficult situations.

Qualities of a Good Team Player

Individuals who exhibit particular characteristics and actions, such as those that contribute to a healthy team dynamic, are the foundation of productive teamwork. The following are some of the most important characteristics of a good member of a team:

Communication

Strong communicators are always present in good team members. They make an effort to understand the perspectives of others, communicate their thoughts concisely, and offer useful criticism.

Reliability

The members of the team know they can rely on trustworthy folks. They keep the promises they make, keep the deadlines they set, and carry out the obligations that have been given to them.

Adaptability

Unanticipated obstacles are a common occurrence for teams. An excellent member of the team is flexible and adaptable and is willing to modify their behavior in response to shifting conditions.

Respect

A strong team is built on the foundation of mutual respect for one another. Team players show respect for their teammates and value the viewpoints and contributions of their other teammates.

Collaboration

Working together as a unified unit is necessary for successful collaboration. Team players are those who are willing to work together, share credit, and prioritize the team's aims over their interests.

Problem-Solving

Strong members of a team are problem-solvers who take the initiative. They recognize problems and participate in the process of locating solutions.

Positive Attitude

The morale of the team may be boosted by having a positive attitude. Perspectives that are positive and constructive are maintained by team players.

Developing Teamwork Skills

Self-improvement is an ongoing activity that must be engaged in if one wants to develop into an effective member of a team. The following are some methods that will assist you in developing and improving your abilities to operate in a team:

Understand Team Goals

Get a good grasp on the aims and expectations of the team, as well as the part you play in working toward reaching those goals.

Active Listening

Pay close attention to what the rest of your team is saying. Inquire into matters that need to be clarified and make an effort to comprehend their points of view.

Effective Communication

Clear and straightforward expression of your ideas and opinions is required. Avoid using jargon or terminology that is highly technical since it may cause people to become confused.

Build Relationships

Cultivate constructive relationships with the members of your team. Learn about their strong points and their areas of improvement, as well as their preferred method of communication.

Collaborative Problem-Solving

When problems develop, you should work together with the rest of your team to identify solutions. It is important to encourage free dialogue and group brainstorming sessions.

Share Credit

Recognize the efforts that your fellow team members have put forth. Try to avoid claiming all of the credit for the successes of the group.

Conflict Resolution

Take immediate and productive action to address any problems or disagreements that arise. Concentrate on locating areas of agreement and potential solutions.

Feedback

Be kind both while giving and receiving comments. The team can improve and mature as a result of receiving constructive comments.

Take Initiative

Take the initiative to contribute in a positive way to the success of the team. Keep an eye out for ways you may provide value, and if the situation calls for it, volunteer to take on more duties.

Time Management

You need to be able to efficiently manage your time to achieve the deadlines and fulfill the promises you made to the team.

Stay Positive

Always keep a good attitude, especially when confronted with difficult circumstances. A constructive viewpoint may invigorate and encourage the members of your team.

Learn from Experience

Consider the experiences you've shared with your team. Determine the areas in which you excelled and the ones in which you have room for improvement.

Common Teamwork Challenges and Solutions

The rewards of working together are great, but there are also difficulties to overcome. The following are some typical problems that teams confront, as well as solutions to those problems:

Poor Communication

Misunderstandings and arguments can result from poor communication. The answer is to make sure everyone on the team is on the same page.

Lack of Participation

It's possible that some of your teammates aren't working as hard as they should.

The answer is to foster a friendly environment where everyone feels at ease discussing views.

Conflict

Team environments always lead to conflicts. Quickly and constructively addressing issues, with a focus on solutions that benefit the team, is the best course of action.

Unequal Workload

It's not uncommon for some team members to take on more than their fair share of responsibilities. The answer is to divide up work clearly and equitably.

Lack of Direction

When teams lack direction or a strong leader, they may struggle to achieve their goals. Create well-defined goals and assign responsibilities, if required.

Time Management

If members of your team have trouble keeping track of time, you may have trouble meeting deadlines. Timelines should be reasonable, and good time management techniques should be encouraged.

Chapter 18

Time Management: How to Be the Boss of Your Time

Our success, happiness, and contentment in life all depend on how effectively we manage our most precious resource: time. Mastering the skill of time management is equivalent to taking control of your life in a world where demands and diversions are constant. Making the most of the time you have is more important than wishing for more of it to appear in your day. In this chapter, written with teens in mind, we'll go on an adventure to discover the foundations of effective time management, arming you with the knowledge and skills you'll need to rule your schedule with an iron fist.

The Priceless Nature of Time: How to Be the Boss of Your Time

"Time is what we want most, but what we use worst." - William Penn

When you're a teenager, it's easy to feel that time is both plentiful and scarce. There have been major shifts in your daily activities, obligations, and priorities. Finding a happy medium between academics, extracurriculars, friends, and hobbies may be difficult. This is why it's so important to learn how to effectively manage your time while you're still a teenager. It helps you feel in charge and secure as you navigate the chaotic teen years, setting you up for future success.

The Teenage Time Dilemma

Teenagers have special time management problems. On the plus side, you might have greater freedom to pursue your own goals and interests. However, academic and extracurricular responsibilities can increase. In addition, if you let it, the pull of digital gadgets, social media, and entertainment will eat up huge chunks of your time.

The adolescent years are formative and exploratory, but they also need disciplined time management. How, therefore, can you take charge of your time during this exciting period?

Understanding Your Priorities

Prioritizing your responsibilities is a necessary first step before implementing any time management tactics. Some things you could put first as a teen are:

Academics

Keeping up with your studies, finishing your work, and getting ready for your tests.

Extracurricular Activities

Participating in extracurricular activities, such as sports, the arts, or clubs.

Social Life

Taking part in social events and getting to know those around you better.

Personal Development

Discovering and pursuing your interests, passions, and aspirations.

Digital Devices

Getting around the Internet, with all its social networks, entertainment options, and educational resources.

Well-Being

Maintaining a healthy body and mind via active pursuits, rest, and attention to oneself.

You can better manage your time once you know what you want to focus on.

Principles of Effective Time Management for Teens

As an adolescent, you need to adopt certain beliefs and habits to take charge of your time:

Goal Setting for Teens

Setting objectives might help you make better use of your time. It might help you prioritize your tasks and stay on track with your goals. Teens often set objectives related to academic performance, personal development, and college applications. Create SMART (Specific, Measurable, Achievable, Relevant, and Time-bound) objectives that span both the near and far futures.

For instance, "I will improve my math grade from a B to an A- by the end of this semester through consistent study and seeking help as needed" is a SMART goal.

Prioritization Skills

Prioritization is a key component of efficient time management. Learn to distinguish between what must be done immediately and what can wait. The Eisenhower Matrix is a useful tool for prioritizing your work (urgent/important, not urgent/important, urgent/not urgent, not urgent/not important). Prioritize the jobs that fall into the "urgent and important" column.

For teens, this can entail prioritizing study time over time spent with friends or finishing schoolwork before watching TV.

Creating a Teen-Friendly Schedule

Teenagers tend to have their routines. Developing a routine that works with your energy levels is crucial. A lot of youngsters are morning people, but others work better at night. If at all feasible, structure your day around when you're at your most productive.

To further aid in organization and progress, think about making use of digital tools or applications created specifically for time management and study preparation.

Saying No with Diplomacy

Teenagers, in particular, need to practice saying "no." It's fun to try new things and meet new people, but if you take on too much, you may end up feeling overwhelmed and burned out. When your plate is already full, politely refuse new commitments and explain that you need to prioritize your present obligations.

Time Blocks for Focus

The term "time blocking" refers to a method whereby distinct chunks of time are set aside for certain endeavors. You may, for instance, set out a certain amount of time each day for studying, fun, and rest. This method allows you to maintain concentration and avoids the overlapping of duties.

Practical Time Management Strategies for Teenagers

Let's get into some teen-friendly, hands-on techniques for managing your time effectively:

Create a Weekly Schedule

Make a weekly plan that includes all of your obligations, including class time, extracurriculars, study time, and leisure time. Be careful to schedule time to rest and rejuvenate. Estimate the time commitment of each work carefully.

Set Daily Goals

Start each day with a plan for what you hope to accomplish. These targets should fit in with your priorities and the time you have available.

Use Time Management Apps

Make use of teen-oriented time management software and applications. You may use these applications to organize your time, remind you of important dates, and keep tabs on your progress. Todoist, Trello, and Google Calendar are just a few of the many popular choices.

Minimize Digital Distractions

Despite their usefulness, digital devices may be serious time wasters. Limit your use of electronic devices and applications before bed and while trying to get some work done.

Study Techniques

Make the most of your time spent studying by using efficient study methods. The Pomodoro Technique (work in 25-minute blocks, with 5-minute pauses) is effective in increasing focus and memory recall.

Regularly Review and Adjust

It's important to evaluate your methods of time management regularly and make any necessary improvements. Priorities and obligations shift as you go through life.

Chapter 19

Money Matters: Financial Skills for Freedom

Your ability to earn and save money is directly correlated to your level of freedom, happiness, and longevity. You may be a teenager who thinks that money is for grownups, but it's never too early to start learning the skills that will lead to financial independence. In this chapter, we'll go over some of the fundamentals of personal finance to help you make better decisions and move closer to your goals.

The Importance of Financial Literacy

"The lack of money is the root of all evil." - Mark Twain

Being financially literate sets you up for a lifetime of sound financial decision-making. It's about learning the fundamentals of personal finance, from making and keeping money to investing and spending. Many graduates of today's schools are unprepared to handle their finances since financial education is rarely emphasized in the classroom.

Teenagers are in a prime position to learn valuable lifelong financial skills and information. The foundation you lay today can serve you well in the future, whether you want to use your savings for higher education, launch a business, or just enjoy a comfortable retirement.

Financial Independence and Freedom

Envision a day when you are financially secure enough to follow your dreams, take that trip of a lifetime, or donate to the organizations that matter to you. To be financially free doesn't require a lot of money; rather, it implies being able to manage your resources in a way that supports your beliefs and aspirations.

If you want to be an entrepreneur, an artist, a scientist, or do anything else for a living, financial independence frees you from having to worry about money so you may pursue your passion. You can also better prepare for the future and withstand any storms that may come your way.

Building Financial Foundations as a Teenager

Understanding the fundamental concepts of financial management is essential before delving into the intricacies of money management. You may build a solid financial foundation on these tenets:

1. Budgeting: The Art of Financial Planning

A budget is a strategy for allocating and spending your money. It's a useful tool for controlling your spending habits and setting aside money for important goals. Putting together a budget may seem like a big task, but it just entails:

Identifying Income:

Add up all the money you get regularly, such as presents, allowances, and profits from part-time work.

Tracking Expenses:

Spend a month tracking your expenditures to get a feel for where your money is going. Separate the mandatory costs (like housing and transportation) from the discretionary ones (like dining out).

Setting Financial Goals:

Choose where you want your money to go, whether it's a one-time purchase, a rainy-day fund, or long-term investing.

Creating a Budget:

Make a plan for how much money will go into each area based on your income and outgoings.

Monitoring and Adjusting:

Maintain financial discipline by checking in on your budget regularly. If your income or spending fluctuates, readjust accordingly.

Rather than forcing you to limit your spending, a budget should provide you with the information you need to make wise decisions about your money and achieve your goals.

2. Saving and Investing: Building a Secure Future

To ensure one's financial stability, saving and investing are crucial. They entail budgeting for both immediate expenses and distant aspirations. Here's a guide for young adults on how to save and invest:

Emergency Fund:

Create a savings account right away. This fund is intended to be used for unforeseen costs such as medical care or vehicle maintenance. The recommended goal is three to six months of savings.

Long-Term Goals:

Think about things like going to college, establishing a company, and purchasing a home. Start putting away money regularly, even if it's just a few dollars, toward these objectives right away.

Investing:

As your savings grow, you may want to think about putting some of it to work for you by investing. There is inherent risk in investing, but the potential rewards outweigh that risk over time. Stocks, bonds, and mutual funds are just some of the financial vehicles you can research.

3. Avoiding Debt: Managing Borrowing Wisely

The burden of debt may be cut both ways. Responsible use of credit can pave the way to realizing dreams like funding further education or buying a home. However, mounting credit card or loan debt with sky-high interest rates can cause serious financial difficulties.

Managing debt responsibly is a skill that should be ingrained in teenagers early on. Don't take on more debts than you need, and if you do, have a solid strategy for paying them back.

Practical Financial Skills for Teenagers

Now that you have a firm grasp on financial basics, let's dive into some more advanced topics about money management:

Track Your Expenses

Budgeting is the first step. Don't forget to tally up every single penny you spend over the next 30 days. By doing so, you may assess your current spending patterns and determine where you can make reductions or where more dollars might be better allocated.

Set Clear Financial Goals

Set both short-term and long-term financial objectives. Want to put money down for a vehicle, school, or a trip of a lifetime? Establishing concrete objectives provides focus and direction for your personal finance journey.

Create a Teen-Friendly Budget

Make a spending plan that takes into account your situation as a teenager. Plan for mandatory costs like tuition, transportation, and savings, as well as optional ones like entertainment.

Save Regularly

Learn to save regularly. When you are paid, whether it's an allowance, a paycheck, or a present, put some of it away in savings. If you want to be consistent with your savings, it's best to automate it.

Learn About Investing

Put forth the effort to become financially literate and investigate various investment vehicles, such as stocks, bonds, and mutual funds. Although learning the fundamentals of investing may not be high on your list of teen concerns, it will serve you well in the long run.

Understand Debt

Learn the ins and outs of various debts and their consequences. If you must use a credit card, do so with caution and pay off your debt in full each month to avoid paying exorbitant interest fees.

Seek Financial Education

Think about enrolling in a personal finance course or reading a book. Teenagers have access to a wealth of helpful financial education materials on the Internet and via mobile applications.

Chapter 20

Goal Setting: How to Plan for Your Bright Future

Take a look into the future and see yourself having accomplished all of your most important goals. It's not some unattainable ideal; rather, it's a reality you can create through focused effort. In this chapter, we'll dive into the science and art of goal-setting so that you may design a life that's rich with accomplishments and personal growth.

The Power of Goals

"Goals are the road maps that guide you to your destination. Cultivate the habit of setting clearly-defined written goals; they are the road maps that guide you to your destination." - Roy T. Bennett

Targets are like bright stars that help you find your way. They show you the way, motivate you to take action, and take you places you never would have imagined going. No matter how big or tiny they are, objectives provide focus and motivation. Setting meaningful goals is a superpower that may have a significant impact on your life as a teenager.

Setting the Stage for Success

Setting goals helps you focus on the result. They help you turn intangible aspirations into attainable goals. Achieving success requires setting goals, which entails

Increase Motivation:

The pursuit of one's goals is what fuels one's enthusiasm and motivates one to act. They give you the strength to keep going when the going gets tough.

Boost Confidence:

Achieving any objective, no matter how modest, may boost your self-esteem. As you take on bigger and riskier endeavors, your confidence in yourself will prove to be invaluable.

Enhance Focus:

Setting objectives allows you to focus on what is most important. They help you concentrate and stay on task.

Measure Progress:

Setting and working toward goals gives you something to strive towards. You may monitor your progress and alter your approach accordingly.

Foster Resilience:

Problems and failures occur frequently in human existence. Setting and achieving goals teaches you to be flexible and resilient in the face of setbacks.

Goals for Different Aspects of Life

Your life goals might encompass many different things. Those spheres of influence may be rather expansive.

Academic Goals:

These targets might include improving grades, securing financial aid, or getting into a certain school.

Personal Development Goals:

Specifically, the focus here is on bettering oneself. Acquiring a new skill, increasing your efficiency, and fortifying your self-assurance are all examples.

Career and Professional Goals:

Career goals can be established as early as the adolescent years. Internships, temporary jobs, and general career exploration might all fall under this category.

Financial Goals:

Establishing monetary objectives paves the way to financial autonomy. Saving for a rainy day, getting your business off the ground, or paying for education all require well-defined financial objectives.

Health and Wellness Goals:

Your health and happiness come first. Healthy, well-rounded living includes efforts toward exercise, nutrition, and emotional well-being.

Relationship Goals:

Relationship building is an ongoing process that requires constant attention. The purpose may be to learn something new, deepen existing relationships, or meet new people.

The SMART Goal Setting Framework

The SMART goal-setting method is effective. The acronym SMART stands for:

Specific:

Set an exact intention. In other words, don't just aim to "get better at sports." In its place, you may write, "I want to get better at soccer by dribbling and shooting every day for 30 minutes."

Measurable:

Figure out how you'll know when you've arrived at your destination. Keeping a tally of grades, fitness sessions, or even money saved are all examples.

Achievable:

Make sure it's a goal you can achieve. While it's good to have lofty aspirations, if they're too far out of reach they might be discouraging. Think about what you can do with what you have right now.

Relevant:

Your objective should reflect your deepest beliefs. It ought to be something you're enthusiastic about and invested in.

Time-bound:

Put a date on it: your desired deadline. A sense of urgency is created, and you can maintain concentration. Getting a 90% or better in math before the conclusion of the semester is one such goal.

Chapter 21

Decision-Making and Emotional Management: Your Inner Compass

Your decisions in life will determine your course and mold who you become. When you're a teenager, you're making a lot of decisions and under a lot of pressure. You can better handle the emotional ups and downs of adolescence and make decisions that are in line with your beliefs if you've honed your decision-making and emotional management abilities.

The Art of Decision-Making

"In any moment of decision, the best thing you can do is the right thing. The worst thing you can do is nothing." - Theodore Roosevelt

The value of being able to make decisions for oneself cannot be emphasized. You have to make choices, both big and small, every day, from how to dress to how to handle a friendship dispute. A more methodical approach to decision-making can aid in the selection of actions that promote development and happiness.

The Decision-Making Process

You can navigate even the trickiest options with the help of a well-thought-out decision-making process. A condensed version is as follows:

Identify the Decision:

Identify the exact nature of the choice you must make. Realize the situation and the stakes.

Gather Information:

It's important to gather all the data you can before making a call. Research, advice-seeking, and introspection are all viable options.

Consider Your Values:

Think about what you hold dear and why. In what ways do the varying possibilities accommodate your most vital concerns?

List Pros and Cons:

Make a chart comparing the benefits of each potential decision. You may use this to think through the many scenarios.

Make the Decision:

Make a decision based on your research. Have faith in your good sense and be ready to own the results.

Take Action:

Put your plan into action and do what you know has to be done.

Reflect and Learn:

After making a choice, it's important to sit back and evaluate what just happened. How did you grow as a result of this?

Factors That Influence Decisions

Many circumstances can impact the choices you make. Among the most typical are:

Peer Pressure:

Trying too hard to please others might cause you to compromise your morals and act in ways that go against who you truly are.

Emotions:

When you're feeling angry, scared, or too excited, it might be difficult to think clearly. The ability to control one's emotions is a prerequisite to making rational choices.

Values and Beliefs:

The choices you make reflect your own unique set of values and ideas. Having a firm grasp on your values allows you to make decisions that are true to who you are.

Consequences:

The probable outcomes of a choice are crucial factors to consider. Both the immediate and long-term effects need to be considered.

Emotional Management: Navigating the Roller Coaster

"Emotions are like waves. You can't stop them from coming, but you can choose which ones to surf." - Jonatan Mårtensson

Extreme feelings and the difficulty of controlling them are common during adolescence. Your well-being and your ability to make sound choices depend on your ability to ride out this emotional roller coaster.

Recognizing Emotions

Recognizing and accepting your feelings is the first step towards mastering your emotions. Feelings can be expressed in several ways, including mental processes, bodily experiences, and actions. Keep in mind:

Physical Sensations:

What physical reactions do various states of mind elicit in you? Do you have a pounding heart, a knot in your stomach, or feelings of tension?

Thoughts:

In what ways do your ideas mirror your feelings? Do they incline toward extremes, or are they reasonable and balanced?

Behaviors:

How do you handle yourself when you're feeling sad, angry, happy, etc.? Do you isolate yourself, become angry, or try to hurt yourself?

Strategies for Emotional Management

Emotion management does not include stifling feelings but rather understanding and appropriately responding to them. The emotional difficulties of adolescence can be overcome with the following techniques:

Mindfulness and Meditation:

These techniques help you learn to keep an objective eye on your inner world. Emotional intelligence and control are fostered.

Healthy Coping Mechanisms:

Find more positive ways to deal with your emotions instead of abusing substances or hurting yourself. What works for one person may not work for another, so it's important to find what does.

Emotional Expression:

Try to communicate your feelings healthily. Releasing pent-up emotions can be accomplished by journaling, talking to a therapist, or participating in physical exercises like jogging or yoga.

Problem-Solving:

Use your problem-solving talents to get to the bottom of how you feel when presented with a difficult scenario. More efficient and long-lasting answers may emerge as a result.

Chapter 22

Emergencies and Safety: Be Prepared, Be Safe

Even though most days are routine, an unforeseen emergency might arise at any time since life is unpredictable. When it comes to protecting yourself and the people around you, being ready and understanding what to do may make all the difference. In this chapter, we'll talk about how important it is for teenagers to be prepared for emergencies and know how to be safe in dangerous situations.

The Importance of Emergency Preparedness

"By failing to prepare, you are preparing to fail." - Benjamin Franklin

Natural catastrophes, accidents, medical emergencies, and other unforeseen events in daily life are only a few examples. We can only hope for the best, but it's important to be ready for the worst in case it happens. Having the skills, supplies, and frame of mind to deal with a crisis effectively requires preparation.

Why Teenagers Need to Be Prepared

As an adolescent, you develop a sense of self-reliance and maturity. Even if you can't always influence the world around you, there are times when being well-prepared makes all the difference:

Home Alone:

You may be spending a lot of time at home alone or looking after younger siblings. It is critical to be prepared for unexpected events.

Independent Travel:

You could start using public transportation to and from school, part-time jobs, and extracurricular activities as your sense of autonomy grows. It's crucial to have everything you need on the road.

Community Engagement:

Volunteering, playing sports, and going to events are all activities that might put you in situations where it's important to be mindful of potential dangers.

The Basics of Emergency Preparedness

There are a few basics to remember when preparing for an emergency:

Risk Assessment:

Get yourself with the types of situations that might arise in your area. Earthquakes, storms, fires, accidents, and medical problems all fall within this category.

Planning:

Make a strategy for your own and your family's protection in case of an emergency. In the event of an emergency, this plan should include how information will be shared, where people will gather, and who will be responsible for what.

Emergency Kit:

Put together a go-bag with supplies including water, nonperishable food, a flashlight, batteries, a first aid kit, and copies of critical documents in case of an emergency. Make sure it's not hard to get to.

Education:

Learn the signs of different situations and how to handle them. In a time of crisis, this information might be crucial.

Responding to Common Emergencies

Fire Safety

Homes, schools, and public buildings are all at risk for fires. Learning what to do in case of a fire is crucial.

Prevention:

Safeguard against fires by using caution around combustibles, never leaving the stove alone, and keeping combustibles at a safe distance from the stove and other heat sources.

Escape Plan:

Create an exit strategy in case of fire. Find all possible exits from your house and label them. Have regular fire drills with your loved ones.

Stop, Drop, and Roll:

Remember to halt, drop to the ground, cover your face with your hands, and roll to put out the flames if your clothing catches fire.

Fire Extinguishers:

Find out where the fire extinguishers are kept and how to utilize them in case of an emergency.

Natural Disasters

Earthquakes, hurricanes, tornadoes, and floods are all possible, but their severity depends on your location. You must be ready for these kinds of things.

Earthquakes:

Put away heavy items, clear the area, and prepare to "Drop, Cover, and Hold On" in the event of an earthquake.

Hurricanes and Storms:

You should stock up on nonperishables, water, flashlights, and a battery-operated weather radio in case of a storm.

Tornadoes:

Be prepared to take cover in a basement or a small, inside room if a tornado is in the area.

Floods:

You shouldn't risk driving through floodwaters since you can't tell how deep they are. If an evacuation is required, you must be ready.

Medical Emergencies

Anyplace, at any moment, medical crises can occur. Learning how to react in a dangerous situation is crucial.

Calling 911:

In the United States, emergency services can be reached by calling 911. Get ready to give details about where you are and what's happening.

First Aid:

Master the fundamentals of first aid, including how to perform CPR, treat wounds, and assist a victim of choking.

Allergies and Medications:

Keep any necessary drugs on hand and inform those around you if you have serious allergies.

Personal Safety

Being prepared for an emergency includes taking measures to ensure your safety in everyday situations:

Online Safety:

Be wary of what information about yourself you post online. Never meet someone you've met online without your parent's knowledge and permission.

Physical Safety:

Always keep an eye out for potential danger, but especially so in new environments. Follow your gut and stay out of harm's way.

Self-Defense:

Take some lessons in self-defense to arm yourself with some tools in the event of a physical confrontation.

Part VI

Technology, Learning, and the Future

Chapter 23

Technology and You: Social Media, Video Games, and More

You can't imagine life without technology, which presents both possibilities and difficulties galore. The online world, including everything from social media to video games, has a significant effect on your life and your future. Responsible online behavior, maximizing technology's educational potential, and becoming ready for a future molded by innovation are all topics we'll discuss in this chapter.

The Digital Revolution

"The digital revolution is far more significant than the invention of writing or even of printing." - Douglas Engelbart

The internet has revolutionized how people communicate, educate themselves, and pass the time. These innovations have the potential to greatly improve people's lives, but they also come with a host of new obligations and risks.

Social Media: The Power and Pitfalls

In terms of how we interact with one another and how we express ourselves, social media sites like Facebook, Instagram, Twitter, and TikTok have been game-changers. They provide a means of communicating with others, exchanging information, and learning about new things. But it's important to think about how they'll affect your health:

Digital Well-Being:

The mental and emotional toll of overindulging in screen time and information that encourages constant comparison is real.

Maintain appropriate distance and put in-person connections first.

Online Safety:

Beware of cyberbullying and always use caution while revealing personal information online. If you witness any form of abuse, please speak up, and be there to help the victims.

Digital Footprint:

Keep in mind that whatever you share online becomes part of your permanent digital record. Make sure your internet presence is representative of who you are and the kind of person you are for colleges and future employers to see.

Video Games: Balancing Entertainment and Responsibility

Video games may be a great source of amusement, education, and team-building exercises. However, problems arise when gaming begins to take precedence over other important activities:

Balance:

Keep a good work/life balance by dividing your time between gaming and things like studying, working out, and hanging out with friends.

Age-Appropriate Content:

Play only games that are appropriate for your age and level of maturity.

Online Interactions:

Always keep an open mind and a kind heart when chatting with other players. Don't be a troll and always keep in mind that your activities online will have real-world repercussions.

Internet Literacy: Navigating the Information Age

While the internet is a wealth of knowledge, it is important to hone your analytical and research abilities to make the most of it.

Fact-Checking:

Before accepting something as true, make sure the source is reliable. Figure out how to identify trustworthy information sources.

Privacy Awareness:

Realize how essential it is to safeguard your personal data when using the internet.

Digital Citizenship:

Respect the rights of others and use appropriate online conduct as a responsible digital citizen.

Harnessing Technology for Learning

"Technology will not replace great teachers but technology in the hands of great teachers can be transformational." - George Couros

Although there are difficulties associated with technology, there are also enormous possibilities for development and improvement. Using technology in the classroom can help you succeed:

Online Learning Platforms

There is a multitude of instructional materials available through online platforms and services. If you want to complement your education and follow your passions, check out online resources like Khan Academy, Coursera, and edX.

Educational Apps

There are a lot of applications out there that can help you learn just about anything. There is probably an app that can help you achieve your academic goals, whether they be in math, languages, or science.

Digital Resources

More books than ever are available at your fingertips thanks to technological advancements like e-books, audiobooks, and online libraries. You may learn a lot more and do research more efficiently with the help of these materials.

Preparing for the Future

It's important to think about how technology will affect your future as you move through the digital world.

Digital Skills

The future employment market will require candidates with strong digital skill sets. Improve your employability by studying a computer language, performing data analysis, or engaging in digital marketing.

Online Safety

Learn how to protect yourself when using the internet. Realize the significance of using robust, one-of-a-kind passwords and the dangers of disclosing sensitive information.

Future Innovations

Keep your mind and your heart open to the possibilities that cutting-edge technologies like AI, VR, and automation provide. The industries and job prospects of the future will be shaped by these breakthroughs.

Chapter 24

Educational Games and Fun Learning: Make Learning a Blast

The process of learning doesn't have to be monotonous. If done properly, it can be loads of fun and interesting. The combination of having fun and learning new things is what makes educational games and other forms of interactive learning so appealing. In this section, we'll delve into the fascinating field of educational games and methods that make education fun and rewarding.

The Joy of Learning Through Play

"The whole purpose of education is to turn mirrors into windows." - Sydney J. Harris

One of the most powerful methods to open doors to new horizons of knowledge is via play, which is why it is integral to the educational process. The way you think about learning may be completely altered by engaging in educational games and other forms of interactive learning.

Why Educational Games Matter

There are several benefits of playing educational games:

Engagement:

Playing games keeps you interested and engaged as you study.

Retention:

Due to the engaging nature of games, players are more likely to remember what they've learned.

Problem-Solving:

The ability to analyze and solve problems is honed when playing several games.

Enjoyment:

Having fun while learning makes it more likely that you'll keep investigating new areas of interest.

Types of Educational Games

Educational games come in a wide range of genres and formats, making them suitable for a wide range of learners.

Puzzle Games:

The games test your ability to think logically and solve problems. Jigsaw puzzles, crosswords, and Sudoku are all great examples.

Simulation Games:

The ability to experience and learn from realistic circumstances is made possible via simulations. Examples include SimCity, The Sims, and aviation simulators.

Math Games:

Mathematical games may make the study of arithmetic and algebra more fun. Popular options include Prodigy and Math Blaster.

Language and Vocabulary Games:

Playing these games is a fun way to improve your language abilities and vocabulary. Games like Scrabble and applications that help you learn a new language come into this category.

Science and Exploration Games:

Video games like the Kerbal Space Program and Universe Sandbox encourage exploration of the outdoors and scientific principles.

History and Culture Games:

Playing games like Civilization and Assassin's Creed is a great way to learn about the past and other civilizations.

Gamification of Learning

The term "gamification" refers to the practice of incorporating characteristics often associated with video games into non-gaming settings, such as classroom instruction. It's a potent method for making education exciting and inspiring.

Achievements:

You can be more productive in your studies if you have the opportunity to earn badges or other awards for achieving certain goals.

Leaderboards:

Making studying into a fun competition with classmates or friends on leaderboards might motivate you to improve.

Progress Tracking:

Charts and graphs may let you see how far you've come, giving you the confidence to keep going.

Effective Strategies for Fun Learning

Adding some levity and interest to your study routine may do wonders for your academic progress. Some ways to make studying more enjoyable:

Set Goals and Challenges

Put yourself to the test by setting some ambitious objectives. Whether you're trying to learn a new language, improve your arithmetic skills, or increase your knowledge of historical events, creating goals that are both challenging and attainable may make the learning process more enjoyable.

Gamify Your Study Routine

Make studying fun by creating a game out of it. Keep yourself motivated with the use of timers, prizes, and internal competitiveness. Set time goals for yourself to do a given number of arithmetic problems or to learn a certain amount of vocabulary.

Explore Interactive Learning Apps

Numerous applications and websites provide opportunities for collaborative study. Tools like Duolingo, Khan Academy, and Quizlet are just a handful that put a new spin on education.

Collaborative Learning

Take advantage of studying with others by turning your sessions into group challenges or quizzes. There are also instructive games and quizzes where you may compete against others.

Embrace Hands-On Activities

Learning may be made more concrete and interesting via experimentation and hands-on exercises. Experimenting in the sciences, making art, or constructing a model are all excellent ways to expand one's knowledge.

Chapter 25

Preparing for College and Beyond: What to Expect

As you near the conclusion of your teenage years, you may find yourself considering your options for further study and beyond. The excitement and the fear of starting college and becoming an adult are equal and opposite. In this chapter, we'll discuss the steps you should take to get ready for college, as well as the trip that lies ahead.

The College Experience

"College is the place where you explore, discover, and create the foundation for your future."

Independence and Responsibility

The move from high school to college is dramatic. You'll have greater freedom in deciding what to study when to study it, and how to study it. Now that you have more leeway in how you spend your time, you must take greater responsibility for your development.

Academic Challenges

College work sometimes requires more independent effort and better time management skills than what one was accustomed to in high school. Courses, instructors, and pedagogical approaches will cover a wide spectrum. The importance of developing good study habits and seeking out academic help when required cannot be overstated.

Career Exploration

You may go further into what fascinates you by attending college. While it is recommended that you have some idea of your professional goals before declaring a major, you should not feel obligated to do so. It's not uncommon for students to switch their concentrations as they progress through school.

Social Growth

College is a place where you may meet interesting individuals from many walks of life. It's a great opportunity to meet new people, expand your social circle, and broaden your educational experience. Make use of these chances to develop yourself socially.

Preparing for Admissions

"Your education is a dress rehearsal for a life that is yours to lead." - Nora Ephron

Application Process

Standardized tests, essays, reference letters, and transcripts may all add extra work to the process of applying to college. Get a head start, do some research on schools that are a good fit for what you want to study, and consult with adults for advice.

Financial Considerations

Knowing how to pay for college is important because of how costly it may be. If you need financial assistance, look for grants, scholarships, and other grants, as well as part-time jobs and internships.

Admissions Tests

Standardized examinations like the SAT or ACT are sometimes a mandatory element of the application process at many universities. Get yourself ready for the tests with the help of study guides and sample tests.

Essays and Personal Statements

Write engaging essays and personal statements that demonstrate who you are and what you hope to achieve. Use your perspective and tone to make an impression.

Life Beyond College

"The journey doesn't end after college; it's just the beginning of the next chapter."

Career Paths

You will begin your professional life after finishing college. Job searching, internships, and further degrees are all viable options. Failure is a necessary part of growth, so pick yourself up and try again.

Continuing Education

Additional training or certification may be necessary for some careers. Think about furthering your education at the graduate level, taking courses to hone your skills, or getting industry-specific credentials.

Personal Growth

You will develop and change and learn new things for the rest of your life. The adult world is always shifting, so it's important to be open to new opportunities, work for your own goals, and be flexible.

Part VII

Conclusion and Extras

Conclusion

The Road Ahead and Your Next Steps

Embrace the Journey

You have successfully navigated this manual and reached its last section. Your time spent here has been an adventure in self-discovery and liberation. You've studied topics like self-improvement, interpersonal dynamics, health, digital literacy, and the process of moving on to higher education and beyond. You've reached a pivotal point between childhood and maturity, and it's important to take stock of your development and plan for the future.

Reflecting on Your Journey

Now is a good time to reflect on the lessons you've gained: You have strengthened your sense of self and your ability to bounce back from adversity. You've laid a solid groundwork for future success by honing crucial life skills like time management and financial literacy. You've done well in the digital era, using your time wisely to further your education and develop yourself. You are ready for the exciting new beginning that college and the world beyond will provide you.

The Road Ahead

Countless new opportunities and adventures are awaiting you down the road. As you go forward into the future, keep your curiosity and desire to learn alive. Keep studying, traveling, and experiencing new things. Define your aspirations and create reasonable targets. Goals give you a sense of where you're going, whether you're talking about your education, your profession, or your development. The obstacles you encounter in life are simply chances to grow intellectually, emotionally, and physically. Don't run from them; instead, confront them squarely. Learn to bounce back from adversity; it's part of the process. Learn to persevere through difficult situations. Invest in your interactions with others; you may learn a great deal from your friends, family, mentors, and classmates. Keep these relationships alive; they will serve as pillars of strength and motivation.

Your Next Steps

After finishing this guide, here are some next actions to think about: Create a plan to achieve your next set of short-term objectives. Don't be afraid to ask for help from others who have been in your shoes. Learn as much as you can about the things that interest you and the world at large. Think About How You Can Give Back to Your Community and the World at Large. Accept Change; show flexibility and openness to new experiences. There might be surprises in store for us in the future.

Final Thoughts

This guide has given you the knowledge and skills you need to thrive throughout this formative adolescent period of growth and self-discovery. The road may be winding and difficult, but know that you are getting closer to the person you want to be with each step you take. You can control your future and make it what you want it to be by cultivating confidence, curiosity, and a dedication to lifelong learning. Welcome to the next stage of the voyage; may it bring you success, fulfillment, and untold opportunities.

I want to say a big thank you for purchasing and reading my book.
If you found value in reading it, please consider sharing it with
friends or family and leaving a review online.
Your feedback and support are always appreciated and allow me
to continue doing what I love.

Bonuses:

Understand Finance

A Teen's Guide to Earning, Saving, and Navigating the Financial World

Teen Study Mastery

Unlocking Academic Success and Confidence with Effective Learning Strategies

Made in the USA
Las Vegas, NV
26 November 2023

81603571R00075